THE YALE DRAMA SERIES

David Charles Horn Foundation

The Yale Drama Series is funded by the generous support of the David Charles Horn Foundation, established in 2003 by Francine Horn to honor the memory of her husband, David. In keeping with David Horn's lifetime commitment to the written word, the David Charles Horn Foundation commemorates his aspirations and achievements by supporting new initiatives in the literary and dramatic arts.

Bathhouse.pptx

JESÚS I. VALLES

Foreword by Jeremy O. Harris

Yale UNIVERSITY PRESS/NEW HAVEN & LONDON

Yale University Press books may be purchased in quantity for educational,
business, or promotional use. For information, please e-mail sales.press@yale
.edu (U.S. office) or sales@yaleup.co.uk (U.K. office).

Set in ITC Galliard and Sabon types by Integrated Publishing Solutions.
Printed in the United States of America.

Library of Congress Control Number: 2024933504
ISBN 978-0-300-27434-9 (paperback : alk. paper)

A catalogue record for this book is available from the British Library.

This paper meets the requirements of ANSI/NISO Z39.48-1992
(Permanence of Paper).

10 9 8 7 6 5 4 3 2 1

Inquiries about performance rights for this play should be directed to Bonnie Davis at
Bret Adams, Ltd, who may be reached at bdavis@bretadamsltd.net.

Dedicated with deepest love to the coven that is Nkenna Akunna, Alexa Derman, and Seayoung Yim, under the tutelage of Julia Jarcho. We are all Raphael.

With deepest gratitude to Claudia Acosta, Fernando Gonzalez, and Kai Thomani Tshikosi, whose voices will always live in the hallways of this play.

In loving memory of Beau Breeden and Tommy Ray Toliver.

Because of Chela and Gerardo.

In memory of every writer and artist martyred in Gaza, in memory of our theater colleagues, Inas al-Saqa and Nour al-Din Hajjaj, in solidarity with the Freedom Theatre in Jenin, in longing for a free Palestine, a plea to you, holding this play in your hands: we can resist and refuse the genocide of Palestinian people with our every breath and action. We must. We, living through the long middle of the revolution, must throw sand in the gears of every imperial death machine. We must.

We use the word "landscape" . . . to refer to a system of relations that are actually too complicated for us to hold in our heads with any concreteness. I think we use this word because it is an abstraction that lets us feel we have a handle on things AND because what it evokes is precisely the opposite of abstraction: a picture you can see, in which sharp, often poignant details combine to form a whole that is also an invitation to tactile adventure. "Landscape" is an abstraction disguising itself as a sensory experience, and vice-versa.

The challenge this semester is to make a landscape for performance. Take us somewhere. We are lost; tempt us with the possibility of knowing where we are, for once. But show us the richnesses, the thicknesses, the peculiarities, the outcroppings that, if truly rendered, will always also interfere with our (that is, your) knowing. . . . On April 15 (our last class), you will conduct a 20-minute LAND-SCAPE PLAY POWERPOINT PRESENTATION (I write these words with a great deal of pleasure at how awful they sound).

    —Julia Jarcho, Syllabus, Brown MFA Playwriting Workshop, Spring 2021

Okay. So, we have to do a PowerPoint?
    —Jesús I. Valles

Contents

Foreword

I remember the smell. Hot chlorine, sticky sweat, viscous lube, and feces old and new met me when I first entered Steamworks in Chicago in 2009. I was eighteen and my friend and I were curious about the men who wandered into the massive building on Halsted, eyes downturned but hungrily peering from beneath caps, gray sweats inviting a peek at what they concealed. There was something beyond shame or transgression in their gaze as they pulled open the large steel door and walked beyond. They walked with a freedom only an appreciation of smut can grant you. As I read *Bathhouse.pptx* for the first time, Jesús I. Valles's words brought those smells and that taste (indescribable to the uninitiated) back to me immediately.

Bathhouse.pptx is a complex, unknowable work because the experience of being a queer person is complex and unknowable. Queer identity, married though it is to the human experience, has remained understudied because it is an identity that morphs with the elemental ease of water from one form to another (liquid, steam, solid) in the blink of an eye. It is right in front of us, below us, behind us, and within us all at any given moment, so the dissection of it as a state of being falters like the element at the core of this play, water, because even its ability to remain liquid is an impermanent state.

Valles began this play while a student in university, and like many of the great queer theorists of our time located the narrative around theorists who demand that the only way we can understand who we are as queer subjects is to also demand that queerness holds all of our histories: cultural, sociopolitical, spiritual. The play takes us into a classroom full of teenagers who are attempting to understand the architecture wherein they learn and the histories that have been erased within its walls: histories of queer Latin men like themselves who once walked these halls riddled with libidinal urges and traumas from global catastrophes that wrecked their communities . . . their only place of solace or sanctuary the bathhouse.

I came to this play at a very particular time in my life. We had just traversed a major global catastrophe that had echoes of one I had only ever read about or seen in films or plays. My libido was at an all-time high after having quarantined myself from intimacies for over a year, and through this PowerPoint presentation that doubled as a play I began to see the prismatic relationship to my present and the pasts I had buried in favor of fretting over my present. It began to work on me as Pushkin's closet dramas did for readers in the nineteenth century. I felt that in times of quarantine and lockdown what better play to celebrate than one that is adventurous and daring on the page and as impossible as could be upon the stage.

It is my great pleasure to invite you to encounter this world Jesús has rendered so playfully here, and perhaps you too will feel as transported as I was through the past, our present, and into the future, in whatever home or bathhouse you encounter it.

Jeremy O. Harris

Production History

Bathhouse.pptx was first workshopped (as *The Shower Play*) at Brown University in December 2021.

Directed by Molly Houlahan

Dramaturgy by Alexa Derman

Cast
    Alfredo Antillon
    Aizhaneya Carter
    Clew
    Alexa Derman
    David Mattar Merten
    Kai Thomani Tshikosi
    Han Van Sciver

Bathhouse.pptx received a workshop and staged reading (as *bathhouse.ppt*) at Brown University's 2022 Writing Is Live Festival.

Directed by Andrew Watring

Dramaturgy by Amanda Macedo

Cast
   Clew
   John Coady
   Benjamin Connor
   Alexa Derman
   Luis Ra Rivera
   Anson Shyu
   Kai Thomani Tshikosi
   Jesús I. Valles
   Rebecca-Anne Whitaker

Bathhouse.pptx received a workshop and staged reading through the Flea in May 2023.

   Directed by Chay Yew

   Dramaturgy by Morgan Jenness

Cast
   Jake Ryan Lozano as THE PRESENTER
   Claudia Acosta as ACTOR 1 (the CHELA track)
   Nic Marrone as ACTOR 2 (the MX. VASQUEZ track)
   Francisco Arcila as ACTOR 3 (the SHAUN track)
   Fernando Gonzalez as ACTOR 4 (the DANIEL track)
   David Mattar Merten as ACTOR 5 (the CARLOS
      track)

Bathhouse.pptx

TIME: When bathhouses have ceased to exist.

PLACE: A tenth-grade honors informative presentation in a cafetorium. A school that was once a bathhouse. The glimmers of a bathhouse at the end of the world.

A NOTE ON CASTING/CHARACTERS: First, no version of this play should exist with an all-white cast. Like, read the play. Go to a bathhouse in Los Angeles. Be for real. Second, invite a version of this play with an entirely trans cast. What might this do for notions of possibility in these places (bathhouses, schools)? Finally, this play can be done with only six actors or with a very large cast—whatever you desire. Below, there are suggested character tracks for actors, but have fun with reconfiguration if needed. Many of the characters are concepts, ideas, grievances, ghosts, or irritations. Please, play inside the garish, the grotesque, the cartoonish, the cruel, the horny, the muscular, the spectral, the heart. This play is a group project for perverts. Go for it. Poppers are strongly encouraged.

THE CHARACTERS

THE PRESENTER: tenth-grader but not really, played by someone who is undeniably an adult; a pervert obsessed with extinctions. Also, in another world, THE ATTENDANT of a bathhouse at the end of the world.

ACTOR I (the CHELA track): plays JUST HAPPY TO HELP! ARE YOU OKAY? / CHELA / SHE'S SELLING THE SHIT OUT OF THIS! / WHAT IT SMELLED LIKE / A WOMAN IN A RI-

DICULOUS PERIOD COSTUME WITH A HORRIBLE ACCENT /
A GHOST UNDER THE STAIRS / LAURA LINNEY, BROUGHT
TO YOU BY THE CDC! / THE BATH BEAUTY

ACTOR 2 (the MX. VASQUEZ track): plays LONGTIME
PUBLIC-SPEAKING TEACHER MX. VASQUEZ, also JUST
VASQUEZ / WILLIAM FEETHAM / THE CDC / A VERY SUP-
PORTIVE PERSON / A CONQUISTADOR! WITH ONE OF
THOSE HATS! Also THE CONQUISTADOR, NOW PLAYING
THE FLOOR and THE CONQUISTADOR WHO WAS THE
FLOOR, NOW STANDING BY THE DOOR / A COCK GOBLIN,
ONE OF HIS BALLS IS ABNORMALLY LARGER THAN THE
OTHER / A GHOST BEHIND THE CLOCK

ACTOR 3 (the SHAUN track): plays JUST DOING THIS FOR A
GRADE / SHAUN / IT HAS BEEN A VERY HARD WEEK /
MAN IN A TOWEL / A GAS CAN, AN EDUCATIONAL FILM,
BROUGHT TO YOU BY QVC / SOME "MEXICAN" THEY
HIRED DOING A TERRIBLE SPANISH ACCENT

ACTOR 4 (the DANIEL track): plays SO NERVOUS ABOUT
THIS, OH GOD / DANIEL / A VERY SMALL CHILD IN THE
AUDIENCE, also A WHOLE-ASS ADULT / HOW IT SOUNDED /
LOOK BUT DON'T TOUCH / A GHOST BEHIND THE DOOR /
A VERY REAL TWINK

ACTOR 5 (the CARLOS track): plays STRONG PICK-ME EN-
ERGY / A PLANT IN THE AUDIENCE, MAYBE AN ACTUAL
PLANT, I DON'T KNOW / CARLOS / A MASCOT EINSTEIN /
A VERY TALL EAGER WHITE MAN THEATER COLLABOR-
ATOR THAT GIVES YOUR THEATER COMPANY THAT AU-
THENTIC "THIS IS A THEATER COMPANY! LOOK AT THIS
QUIRKY, VERY TALL WHITE MAN UP HERE WITH US! MY
GOD! WHAT WILL HE DO!? HE'S GOING TO PLAY A RACIST
IN THIS ONE BUT HE'S ACTUALLY REALLY NICE IN REAL
LIFE. HAVE YOU MET HIS PARTNER? SHE'S FROM VENEZU-

ELA!" ANYWAY, HE'S ACTUALLY REALLY GREAT! PLEASE
ENJOY/ A GHOST UNDER THE RED CUSHIONS

PLAYWRIGHT'S NOTE: I don't know that this play should
be produced. Lately, I think it shouldn't (but I'm not stop-
ping you—you're welcome to try). Sometimes I think this
play is best read alone, or aloud with other queers, pausing
to talk about what sticks, what stings, what irritates, what
sucks, what lands. This is a pandemic play. I started writing
it in January 2021, when I was missing my high school public-speaking classroom the most (I was a high school teacher
for many years), when I was missing the queer clubs and the
bathhouses most, when I was missing theater most. I didn't
think we would return to any of these places again. If we
did, they wouldn't be the same. Many of our students would
be gone, as would many of our colleagues, queens, lovers,
friends, tricks—all the people who populate the landscapes
I love most. *Bathhouse.pptx* is a symptom of loneliness and
longing. It's a paranoid, silly little gay thing. I wrote this play
mostly to make Nkenna Akunna, Mysia Anderson, Alexa
Derman, Julia Jarcho, and Seayoung Yim laugh on Zoom.
I wrote this play because I love Chela. So if you're holding
this play, I hope it's of some use to you. Mostly, I hope you
read it and think about the things you want most. I hope
you remember someone.

Oh, and a slash (/) between words indicates the next
actor should begin speaking their line. Overlapping dialogue.
You know.

FINALLY, A NOTE ON STYLE: This play is a mess. If you
choose to stage it, I hope you have fun. I hope it's wild,
cheap, and inventive. Try not to think too much about the
logics of anything here. Things are because I wanted them
to be. This play is an indulgence. Indulge (me). This play
is shaped like a poorly structured informative speech. The
play's scenes are divided into "Slides." In a full production,

you might have a hastily put-together PowerPoint presentation that signals our transition from scene to scene. The play is a swirl, a little maze: move quickly until you can't, then go again.

Warm-Up, Title Slide

THE PRESENTER *enters, doing warm-ups for speaking—tongue twisters, drinking water, looking over notecards. Nervous gigs.*

THE PRESENTER (*Alone. As a warm-up.*) To articulate
Use the tip of the tongue
And the top of the teeth
And the tip
of the top
of the teeth.
T—T—T—T
Okay

Okay

Uh. I can, uh,
I could go next, Mx. Vasquez. I'd like to present next, if
that's okay. Is / that okay?

LONGTIME PUBLIC-SPEAKING TEACHER MX. VASQUEZ *booms; a voice from a booth. Panopticon.*

LONGTIME PUBLIC-SPEAKING TEACHER MX.
VASQUEZ Sure, if you feel like you're ready. Go ahead.
And the topic is going to be . . . ?

THE PRESENTER Oh. Cleanliness.

Well, bathing.
Baths. / Bathho—

LONGTIME PUBLIC-SPEAKING TEACHER MX.
VASQUEZ   Do you need time to set up visual aids or
Confer with your . . . will you be doing this solo or
With a group?

THE PRESENTER   Uh. Yes.

LONGTIME PUBLIC-SPEAKING TEACHER MX.
VASQUEZ   Yes?

THE PRESENTER   Yes, I'll be doing this alone. But I'll
have some assistance.
So, alone. / With others.

LONGTIME PUBLIC-SPEAKING TEACHER MX.
VASQUEZ   How can you be alone with assistance?
That / doesn't make any sense

THE PRESENTER   They'll just be helping me through
some sections. For extra credit.
We just need a / minute to—

LONGTIME PUBLIC-SPEAKING TEACHER MX.
VASQUEZ   Whatever.

THE PRESENTER   Guys?

JUST HAPPY TO HELP! ARE YOU OKAY?, STRONG PICK-ME
ENERGY, JUST DOING THIS FOR A GRADE enter. *Peers
pour in.*

JUST HAPPY TO HELP! ARE YOU OKAY?   Come on.
He's about to start! (*To* THE PRESENTER, *a machine gun of*

helpfulness.) Do you want some water? You look like you
need some water. I finished the costumes last night, so just
let me—Oh, I also have some questions about your notes?
The order feels—hey, are you okay?

STRONG PICK-ME ENERGY   She's Not. Look at Her.
(*To* THE PRESENTER, *a machine gun.*) You're doing that
thing with your hands again. Look, If you don't want to
do this right now, I'm good to do My Presentation First,
if you want? I can Totally Go First, if you want. I Finished
My PowerPoint on Bolivia Last Night. / Why don't I
just—

JUST DOING THIS FOR A GRADE   Goddamn, I
gotta take *theee* fattest shit.
You guys cool if I go before we start, cuz / I'm fuckin' torn—

JUST HAPPY TO HELP! ARE YOU OKAY?   Stop being
gross! Ugh, / guys are so gross.

JUST DOING THIS FOR A GRADE   It's natural to
take a / shit—

STRONG PICK-ME ENERGY   Actually, in My Research,
I Found That Bolivians Believe That Some People Are
Anal Retentive / as a Result of—

THE PRESENTER   Guys! I'm fine! (*He's not.*) Can we
please / just get back—

SO NERVOUS ABOUT THIS, OH GOD *enters, late.*

SO NERVOUS ABOUT THIS, OH GOD   Uh, sorry
I'm late . . . um, sorry, I just wanted to know . . . Sorry.
Are there—do we have, like, notes
Or anything like—sorry, I just wanted to—uh

THE PRESENTER   No, yeah, yeah for sure. I can share the, uh, yeah.
I got you. I'm—I'm pretty nervous, too.

SO NERVOUS ABOUT THIS, OH GOD   Hehe, yeah. Thanks.

THE PRESENTER   Okay, so the plan is—

They huddle and confer. They are tenth graders, but they aren't. They are actors playing anxieties in the shapes of tenth graders. They consult. Chatter. Anyway, here they go.

THE PRESENTER   . . . which should be fine, since we're all legal and then we'll just switch and I can take it from there. Got it?

JUST DOING THIS FOR A GRADE	SO NERVOUS ABOUT THIS, OH GOD	STRONG PICK-ME ENERGY	JUST HAPPY TO HELP! ARE YOU OKAY?
I guess. Sooner I can get to the bathroom. Fuck, I'm tired—	Shitshit-shitshit Hehe uh . . . yeah . . . shit—	Of Course I've Got It, but Really, if You'd Rather Not—	We got it! Okay, let's go! Are you sure you don't want some water before—

LONGTIME PUBLIC-SPEAKING TEACHER MX. VASQUEZ   Whenever you're ready, I'll start your time. I'm ready. Would you like oral
Or written feedback?

THE PRESENTER   Uh . . . whatever you / think is—

LONGTIME PUBLIC-SPEAKING TEACHER MX.
VASQUEZ   Oral it is! Great! My hand's exhausted.

THE PRESENTER   Uh. Okay.
Guys? Slide!

THE PRESENTER *takes the stage while the group finishes
set-up.*

Slide

Slide 1

Ah, a slide show. Here, a timeline of the history of bathing.

THE PRESENTER   Hello, good afternoon . . . shit . . .
evening. Thank you all for being here, for what is sure to
be a time. A good time . . . fuck . . . Uh, It's an honor
to be with you, as I present this mandatory tenth-grade
honors presentation. I am a tenth grader. Go, class of
2036! And this is My Honors Presentation . . . fuckIal-
readysaidthat . . . Uh . . . Titled: Show(er) & Tell: Cleanliness, Baths and—well. You'll see! . . . shit . . . Before we
begin, we'd like to—I would like to thank the teachers,
friends, and mentors who've come to provide moral support, my parents, who unfortunately could not want to be
with us tonight, and, of course, our good friends from the
federal government, the state legislature, and its various
agencies who are here to kindly . . . to uh . . . fact-check
these presentations . . . for some reason? Okay! We will
begin! Ahem.
. . .
Ahem. We Will Begin!

JUST DOING THIS FOR A GRADE   Oh, shit. Uh,
yeah, an attention getter (*Screams very loudly and briefly.*)
and a shocking fact you may not know: one in every four
Americans this year ALONE will shower. The other 25
percent will be involved in a driving accident. The choice
is Yours! And then I hand it off to the next person.

THE PRESENTER   WOW! Shocking! Now, you may be asking yourself?

JUST HAPPY TO HELP! ARE YOU OKAY?   "HEY, Now, What's THIS Presentation All About?"

THE PRESENTER   Well, I'm here to talk about Cleanliness! How do we do it? Mostly with showers and baths! And why?! As social creatures we desire to be less alone and so to be clean in order to be close to others and not embarrass ourselves with our smells, such as some people in this class . . . Uh . . . Furthermore . . . Oh. Sorry, everyone. My notes seem . . . uh, here is someone else!

THE PRESENTER *shuffles through his notes. The others vamp and vie. They are a lot.*

JUST HAPPY TO HELP! ARE YOU OKAY?   But hey, you may be asking yourself, WIIFM!?! What's in It for Me?! Well, I'll tell you. Not showering can lead to terrible diseases like dysentery, diphtheria . . . (*Off-script, free-word association.*) Dialga, doo-doo, Dimetapp, Diane Lane in *Under the Tuscan Sun,* dead babies. So clearly this topic has social impact, and it is important to learn the history of showers because history repeats itself.

SO NERVOUS ABOUT THIS, OH GOD   But hey, you may be asking yourself, WIIFM?! Oh shit. No, you already—Shit. Uh. Shoot. Yes, I . . . I agree! History is incredibly important to repeat. It's important to look back at way-back-when in order to keep going to now when it's not so way back. Oh, and a Fun Fact: 19 percent of people don't scrub their legs in the shower! And yes, yes they are, / so . . . uh, yeah—

STRONG PICK-ME ENERGY   EXCUSE ME! Hi, I'd actually like to guide us Back to the Facts Here. As a

Student of History, I would argue that we have to begin
with HOW we moved from showering under Natural
Water Formations to the NEXT point in the timeline,
which is SERVANTS. WITH. WATER JUGS. I would
posit that under a Lacanian framework, our relationship
to water and cleanliness is always already ontologically
and epistemologically bound to shame. Aqueous shame,
from the Greek, "AH—GUA," or WA-TER, and / the
ways in which—

THE PRESENTER   (*Finally, landing at a certainty,
wresting some control.*) Ah, yes! Historically, you'll notice
how we evolved through time along with the shower.
Once, we were all beautiful long-haired hour-glassed water-
fall sprites. And then, sometime later, we cut our hair and
become more squarish. Now, given our desire to be with
others, I'd like to shift our focus to communal baths. As
you can see here, ancient Romans / were some—

JUST DOING THIS FOR A GRADE   Oh shit. Yeah,
that's when everybody got real gay, yeah? In this group
shower / situation?

STRONG PICK-ME ENERGY   OOP! UM, Actually,
it's Very Violent to Assume Homosexuality as Early Moti-
vation for Communal Cleansing. In his work, Michel
Foucault Incorrectly / Argues That—

JUST DOING THIS FOR A GRADE   I dunno, man,
whenever I see three or more figures in a shower, I just
assume, like, "Oh hey, look at all those people being gay
in the shower. I bet they're all doing, like, butt stuff. Or
like, docking, throat gapes, / lemon parties, goatses."

THE PRESENTER   ANYWAY, our relationship to
showering and bathing evolves alongside our notions of

cleanliness, which closely follow how we feel about shame. What I will attempt to do here, through this multi-modal presentation, with the aid of my peers, is to show you this relationship, by focusing on some . . . uh, specific artifacts, such as the shower and / the bathhou—

SO NERVOUS ABOUT THIS, OH GOD   But hey, student, you / may—ohshit, I'm sorry, oh wait, that's your part, oh—

JUST HAPPY TO HELP! ARE YOU OKAY?   "HEY, STUDENT," You may be asking yourself, "But who invented the shower?" I'm going to count us down to 5, for our special first "guest." Okaaaaayyyyy. . . . Yeah?
1
2

JUST DOING THIS FOR A GRADE   3, 4, 5! There.

THE PRESENTER   Now, in 1767 AD ENGLAND, WILLIAM FEETHAM!

EVERYONE ALL TOGETHER   WILLLLLLLIIIII-IAAAAAAM FEETHAM!

Slide

Slide 2

WILLIAM FEETHAM *enters. He's a Victorian nightmare, even though it's 1767. He's a terrible British cartoon, the "inventor" of the mechanical bath. While he speaks, the students do a pantomime of what is being explained here; a pantomime of servitude and the early shower. Again, this is a group project for now.*

WILLIAM FEETHAM   It is important to remember that I invented the shower! And why?!
Because children are willful, hideous, clawing things that hate showers and must be made to do so! Shouting and screaming, and shitting about! Filthy! And it is important to remember that perhaps children reveal our desire to revel in what's dirty! But We Mustn't!
Thus, I give you the mechanical bath!

A tenth-grade-assembled diorama/replica of the mechanical bath is revealed.

It is important to remember, of course, that the mechanical bath requires hands—
A maid to fill the water source, a maid to warm the water prior, a servant boy to hold the bucket,
the maid's child perhaps. Servant children are, arguably, less troublesome than one's own children; they have use.
They have stern mothers to ruin the spirit, to quell their want to shit and shout and claw and scream foul, foul

things. They have use. The servant boy, perhaps the child
of the maid, carries a bucket of water. They have use, you
see. Servants and their children.

Servants are needed to clean and it is important to be
clean and it is important that showers be invented and it
is important to corral our filthiest creatures so they may
clean and be cleaned and it is important that "clean" be a
close consonant cousin to the word "cleave," to slit a thing
and to do so with a sharp blade, it is important to ensure
that the water runs hot and to ensure that there are maids
to attend to the water and it is important to know the
names of those who contributed so greatly to the shower
and of course and above all it is important to try not to
think of all the hands needed to make one clean, to never
think of the maid's sad children, and the sad maid, and it
is important that children be scrubbed clean, and cold
scolded, and scalded, and scalloped, and above all to cleave
cleanliness from all the hands that make it, and in doing so
make oneself the standard for what cleanliness is! Thank
you!

WILLIAM FEETHAM *dissipates.*

THE PRESENTER   And then time passes. This is a
transition.
Slide, please.

Slide

Slide 3

The group shuffles, takes in the next slide quickly, and begins.
Costume changes. Places.

THE PRESENTER   The invention of the mechanical
bath ushered in a complex era of commodity and—

LONGTIME PUBLIC-SPEAKING TEACHER MX.
VASQUEZ   (*Reacting to the above, a yawn, a groan.*
Ugh.) Kill me.

THE PRESENTER   Sorrysorrysorrysorry! Here's something exciting! Here! Here's somebody everyone can
agree on! Here to Drive the Point Home, Help Me Welcome Our School Mascot and the Avatar of Innovation,
ALBERT EINSTEIN!

A MASCOT EINSTEIN *bursts through on a light-up hover-*
board holding a giant fucking Nerf water gun.

A MASCOT EINSTEIN   A RAAANGE OF PROD-
UCTS WERE EVOLVING! IN NEW AND EXCITING
DIRECTIONS!
ALL TOGETHER NOW!

EVERYONE ALL TOGETHER   A RAAANGE OF
PRODUCTS WERE EVOLVING! IN NEW AND
EXCITING DIRECTIONS!

A MASCOT EINSTEIN   INTRODUCING! ELEC-
TRIC! HOT! WATER! SHOWERS! TAKE IT AWAY,
MEIN SCHATZ!

A Marilyn Monroe type emerges, SHE'S SELLING THE SHIT
OUT OF THIS!

SHE'S SELLING THE SHIT OUT OF THIS!   Oh my
god! Wow, is that what I think it is? Is that a NEW SEN-
SATION for the LUXURIOUS?

EVERYONE ALL TOGETHER   HOOOOOOOT
WATER OOOOOOOH!

SHE'S SELLING THE SHIT OUT OF THIS!   Wow! So
hot! All this hot water and Ooops! Just little old me! Here
LUXURIATING in my LUXURIOUS hot shower-bath!
OOOOH! Slow, soapy circles—oh my!
Remember, gents: If it's not hot water, you're a poor
person!

EVERYONE ALL TOGETHER   POOOOOR !!!!

A MASCOT EINSTEIN   AND YOU'LL NEVER STOP
THE SPIRIT OF AMERICAN INNOVATION! WATER
JETS! HOT TUBS! SHOWERSHOTS! COLONIC
IRRIGATION!

A MASCOT EINSTEIN *rides away and the group shifts to
return to the PowerPoint.*

THE PRESENTER   OKAY! Yes, excitement! So, clearly,
you can see class . . . is a thing. Throughout time, the
shower becomes a tool of . . . pleasure as exclusion and
Capital . . . ism and um—Oh god—

Shit. I think . . . I'm sorry. Mx. Vasquez, could I take it back? I think I skipped / my thesis—

From above, the voice.

LONGTIME PUBLIC-SPEAKING TEACHER MX. VASQUEZ   I think I missed your thesis statement. The thesis is needed for clarity.
Are we still in the milieu of last week?
When you proposed focusing your / presentation on—

THE PRESENTER   Yes. Yes, it's that. I promise. I just—
Sorry. Okay, pivot.
Now, as Mx. Vasquez always says, anecdotes are the best way to dive into a topic and serve up a thesis. So, uh, here we go. An anecdote: When I was younger and didn't know much about men,
this guy asked me if we could . . . um . . . sorry.
I don't know if I should . . .
The thing is, when I was younger, I was just so eager to please, so so so, so I'm in this bathroom, washing my hands. You know? Cleanliness. And . . . and uh . . . and this guy,
this guy asked if he could / . . . um . . .

JUST DOING THIS FOR A GRADE   You good, / dude?

THE PRESENTER   Yeah, I just think maybe . . . (*aside, to* JUST DOING THIS FOR A GRADE *specifically*) Hey, can you just pull up something else, please? I need—
Mx. Vasquez, do you mind if I skip the anecdote and / jump to—

LONGTIME PUBLIC-SPEAKING TEACHER MX. VASQUEZ   Maybe you shouldn't interrupt your own speech. It can be distracting. For the audience. You don't want them to know you're self-aware.

THE PRESENTER   You mean self-cons/cious?

LONGTIME PUBLIC-SPEAKING TEACHER MX. VASQUEZ   No. "Don't stop now! Keep going!" I am motivating you! Does anyone have a charger? / I'm on 2 percent.

JUST DOING THIS FOR A GRADE *has readied the next slide. A distraction. A thumbs-up.*

THE PRESENTER   Oh, thank god. Slide!

Slide

Slide 4

A slide. A haphazard Google search result—a Mexican worker being sprayed with chemicals at the border. History now, then. The designs of the gas baths, imagined and erected here, then taken elsewhere. History flooding in.

A GAS CAN, AN EDUCATIONAL FILM, BROUGHT TO YOU BY QVC   Mexicans and Cleaning! Here are the facts!
Here's how you delouse a Mexican!
With white.
Let the white run down the body
Cryolite if they're dirty dirty
Dirty Mexicans, nude and full of lice!

THE PRESENTER   Wait. / No, hey, can you—

A GAS CAN, AN EDUCATIONAL FILM, BROUGHT TO YOU BY QVC   Shave their heads, Steam dry the clothes until the shoes melt, and then
Line 'em up for the showers!
Mexicans full of lice and typhus and Mexico
Clean 'em up with gas baths!
Fumigation! Like a house!
A dirty, dirty house in Mexico!
Fumigation on the mandate of the mayor:
"We should bathe and disinfect all the dirty, lousy people who are coming into this country from Mexico . . . We shall continue the work of killing lice and curbing the

effects of immigration at the Mexican border for many
years to come."
Remind them at every turn, conquest begins with the dirt
And their dirty, dirtied selves.
So remember: before you use your Mexicans,
Make sure to sterilize them!
You don't want to get your family sick.

THE PRESENTER   Uh . . .
That is not . . .
I mean, sure, the history of showers, I guess, but / like,
That's not—

JUST DOING THIS FOR A GRADE   Oh—my bad.
It was part of the Google search image results for "baths"
so I just threw it up there.
Hey, you cool if I grab some water real quick? / I'm
fading.

THE PRESENTER   Yeah, of course. All / good . . .

LONGTIME PUBLIC-SPEAKING TEACHER MX.
VASQUEZ   I'm confused. This seems tangential. Un-
related. And you're not doing a great job at signposting
for your audience. I can see they're confused, too. What
do you actually want / to talk about?

THE PRESENTER   No, yeah, I apologize about that.
I don't think I was quite ready to—
(*Oh, actually!*) Actually . . . actually, I think maybe it is
important, before we get to anything salacious, to think
about how often structures of cleanliness and dirt are used
to organize how we treat one another. In class, we've
talked about how shame often makes it difficult to be in
front of others. But we don't talk about how we learn to
feel shame for our very being. The gas baths at the border

are a prime example of how the state deploys racist logics
of purity and danger, dirt, to enforce a public shame that
makes those subjected to the baths disposable, to make
them refuse. For example, when my great-great-grandfather
first came to this country, / he—

THE CDC *interrupts from the audience.*

THE CDC   UH-OH!! Did somebody say racialized
notions of beep boop bap!!? Here we go!
LET'S LOAD UP MY SLIDE /PLEASE!

THE PRESENTER   Um, wait, please . . . /wait, no—

THE CDC   THANK YA! SLIIIIDE!!

Slide

Slide 5

What if a weird, robot nepo baby ran the CDC? Anyway, that's who takes the stage. It's frightening and stupid. THE CDC *begins.*

THE CDC   Hello, I'm the CDC! The Centers for Disease Control! Or the Christian Defense Coalition! Just depends who's in office that day! That's a little joke!

THE PRESENTER   Uh . . . hello. Thank you so much for being here to uh . . . adjudicate? Um . . . Would you mind if I just finish my present/ation and . . . Mx., Mx. Vasquez, c-c-could we—

THE CDC   Thank You Soooo Much! for bringing such important issues to the table today, young man! Now more than ever! I mean, Water?! Amiright!? Wow!
So, because this is an educational event, we'd like to Take This Opportunity to educate with excerpts from *Love (in the Time of) Cholera!*, a new public works project from the greater cultural arts division of the CDC co-sponsored by Gilead as part of our water-diversity initiative.
You like theater, right, kid? GOOD! Here we go!

Two actors enter. One of them is SOME "MEXICAN" THEY HIRED DOING A TERRIBLE SPANISH ACCENT *and other is* A WOMAN IN A RIDICULOUS PERIOD COSTUME WITH A HORRIBLE ACCENT. *Ah! Ah! They're acting.*

SOME "MEXICAN" THEY HIRED DOING A TER-
RIBLE SPANISH ACCENT   (*In character.*) "To him
she seemed so beautiful, so seductive, that he could not
understand why everyone did not go mad with the gold
of her laughter! But he did not dare approach her for fear
of destroying the spell!"

A WOMAN IN A RIDICULOUS PERIOD COSTUME
WITH A HORRIBLE ACCENT   (*In character.*) "When
a woman decides to sleep with a man, there is no wall she
will not scale, no moral consideration she will not ignore!
There is no God worth worrying about!" (*She breaks
character.*)
Okay, and then is this when I rip my bodice off? Or /
should I—

THE CDC   Yeah, this is when you rip the bodice off and
then—Michael? She'll rip her bodice off and let's have you
run at her, tackle her to the ground, INTO the kiddie
pool, and then we'll do the song.
Let's try it and go into the song!

A WOMAN IN A RIDICULOUS PERIOD COSTUME
WITH A HORRIBLE ACCENT   (*Out of character.*)
Okay, I'm just gonna take it from . . . okay, okay. (*In
character.*) "There is no God worth worrying about!"

A chorus of people with cholera enter. A group number. A
CHORUS LINE! 5, 6, 7, 8!

A CHOLERA CHORUS LINE! 5, 6, 7, 8!   WE'VE GOT
CHOLERA! WE'VE GOT CHOLERA! YES, WE DO!
WE'VE GOT CHOLERA! WE'VE GOT CHOLERA!
HOW 'BOUT YOU?!
BOIL ALL THAT WATER, BOIL IT TWICE!
BOIL IT AND BOIL IT, IT TASTES REALLY NICE!
BUT IF YOU FORGET TO BOIL IT FOR DRINKING

GOD, THEN YOU'LL DIE! OH, WHAT WERE YOU
THINKING?!
SO BOIIIIIIILL
YOUR WAAAATEER
TODAAAAAAAAAAAAAAAYYYY!!
CHOLERA!
BLERRGGGGGGGHHHHHHHHHH!!!

THE CDC   Great. So then all the cholera people vomit
around the two lovers in the kiddie pool and they all die
in a pile. That's great. Thank you all so much for coming
to support our public-speaking students. I believe the
children are our future, teach them well and remember—
Cholera remains an insidious scourge.
So, are there any questions at this time that a pamphlet
can't answer?

A VERY SMALL CHILD IN THE AUDIENCE *asks a question.*

A VERY SMALL CHILD IN THE AUDIENCE   Uh.
Hi, sir. I'm a very small child in the audience, and gee, I
was just wondering,
What if my city issues a boil-water notice?
Can I still shower with that water?

THE CDC   Uh. Sure. Why . . . why wouldn't you
shower?
It's just drinking and cooking that . . . uh . . . that causes
problems?
Okay. Well, I guess, that answers all of the questions.
Goodbye!

THE CDC *slowly exits on a shitty Tesla jet-pack.*

THE PRESENTER   Um . . . thank you. To uh, our
esteemed guests from the CDC . . . for continuing to . . .
continue. As I was / saying—

A VERY SMALL CHILD IN THE AUDIENCE   Hi.

THE PRESENTER   Hello.

A VERY SMALL CHILD IN THE AUDIENCE   Do
you mind if I ask my question up there? It'll just be a
minute. Please?

THE PRESENTER   Okay, sure. Hey, but then I really
need to get back / to my pres—

A VERY SMALL CHILD IN THE AUDIENCE   Okay.
Next slide, please.

A VERY SMALL CHILD IN THE AUDIENCE *adorably gets up
onstage.*

Slide

Slide 6

In this slide, a Mexican baby, bathing in a giant metal tub.

A VERY SMALL CHILD IN THE AUDIENCE   Hi.
I'm a Very Small Child. Well, not really, but that's where
I want to speak from. Because of this water crisis in my
city. My mother is from a very small ranch in Chihuahua,
Mexico. And when I was a very, very small child she would
tell me that when she was a very small child her very large
mother would bathe her in one of these very large metal
tubs. My grandmother would boil medium-sized pots of
water to pour them into the very large tub, like this one,
for a hot bath. A clean child takes time, but when you
don't have much, cleaning children must be done fast and
rough, with hot water, because if you were a very, very
poor person cleaning other people's homes, the best thing
you could have was a very, very clean child. And because
most dust in people's homes is just skin, the best way to
ensure a clean home is to scrub your children very, very
hard, until they are red, so they don't make a mess in other
people's homes and in your own. There are pictures of me,
red, somewhere in a tub like this one, from when I was a
very, very small child, unimaginably small in comparison
to the present.

Anyway, my city just got a boil-water notice and we
stocked up as much water as we could, but we still don't
have any clean running water, and I just wanted to know if

I should boil the water before I bathe with it, or if it's okay to just wash myself / with it—

From the audience enters A VERY TALL EAGER WHITE MAN THEATER COLLABORATOR THAT GIVES YOUR THEATER COMPANY THAT AUTHENTIC "THIS IS A THEATER COMPANY! LOOK AT THIS QUIRKY, VERY TALL WHITE MAN UP HERE WITH US! MY GOD! WHAT WILL HE DO!? HE'S GOING TO PLAY A RACIST IN THIS ONE BUT HE'S ACTUALLY REALLY NICE IN REAL LIFE. HAVE YOU MET HIS PARTNER? SHE'S FROM VENEZUELA!" ANYWAY, HE'S ACTUALLY REALLY GREAT! PLEASE ENJOY. *That's his name. Okay, here he is!*

A VERY TALL EAGER WHITE MAN THEATER COLLABORATOR THAT GIVES YOUR THEATER COMPANY THAT AUTHENTIC "THIS IS A THEATER COMPANY! LOOK AT THIS QUIRKY, VERY TALL WHITE MAN UP HERE WITH US! MY GOD! WHAT WILL HE DO!? HE'S GOING TO PLAY A RACIST IN THIS ONE BUT HE'S ACTUALLY REALLY NICE IN REAL LIFE. HAVE YOU MET HIS PARTNER? SHE'S FROM VENEZUELA!" ANYWAY, HE'S ACTUALLY REALLY GREAT! PLEASE ENJOY   Wait, okay, I actually totally have a story like this too, kind of! Wait, hold on. I'm gonna get up there real quick with you.
Hold on.
Okay. Slide / please.

That white man's up there now.

THE PRESENTER   No. SIR?! NO!

Slide

Slide 7

A VERY TALL EAGER WHITE MAN THEATER
COLLABORATOR THAT GIVES YOUR THEATER
COMPANY THAT AUTHENTIC "THIS IS A THE-
ATER COMPANY! LOOK AT THIS QUIRKY, VERY
TALL WHITE MAN UP HERE WITH US! MY GOD!
WHAT WILL HE DO!? HE'S GOING TO PLAY A
RACIST IN THIS ONE BUT HE'S ACTUALLY
REALLY NICE IN REAL LIFE. HAVE YOU MET
HIS PARTNER? SHE'S FROM VENEZUELA!" ANY-
WAY, HE'S ACTUALLY REALLY GREAT! PLEASE
ENJOY   Hi, everyone! / I'm—
I just want to say that you're—Wow, this presentation is
just really forcing me to think
So Many Things right now.
Sorry, it's just that I really love showers.

From the audience, A VERY SUPPORTIVE PERSON *supports
very loudly.*

A VERY SUPPORTIVE PERSON   No, no, stop it, don't
apologize. I totally get it.
You know what? Do you want me to go up there with
you?

A VERY TALL EAGER WHITE MAN THEATER
COLLABORATOR THAT GIVES YOUR THEATER
COMPANY THAT AUTHENTIC "THIS IS A THE-
ATER COMPANY! LOOK AT THIS QUIRKY, VERY

TALL WHITE MAN UP HERE WITH US! MY GOD!
WHAT WILL HE DO!? HE'S GOING TO PLAY A
RACIST IN THIS ONE BUT HE'S ACTUALLY
REALLY NICE IN REAL LIFE. HAVE YOU MET
HIS PARTNER? SHE'S FROM VENEZUELA!" ANY-
WAY, HE'S ACTUALLY REALLY GREAT! PLEASE
ENJOY   Oh my god, would you? Actually, that would be
really, really great.
It would make this whole thing feel less lonely.

THE PRESENTER   No! No, what are you / doing?!
Stop it!

A VERY SUPPORTIVE PERSON   I'm aiding a person
in pain. Can you please hold space for that?

THE PRESENTER   That's not what this / is about—

A VERY SUPPORTIVE PERSON   Have you ever felt
lonely?

THE PRESENTER   Well, yeah, /but—

A VERY SUPPORTIVE PERSON   So, here we are.
With you. Onstage. See? When we help ourselves, we help
others. I'm up here now. For US.
(*Pivoting to* A VERY TALL EAGER . . .)
For you. I totally feel you. So Much to Think About.

A VERY TALL EAGER WHITE MAN THEATER
COLLABORATOR THAT GIVES YOUR THEATER
COMPANY THAT AUTHENTIC "THIS IS A THE-
ATER COMPANY! LOOK AT THIS QUIRKY, VERY
TALL WHITE MAN UP HERE WITH US! MY GOD!
WHAT WILL HE DO!? HE'S GOING TO PLAY A
RACIST IN THIS ONE BUT HE'S ACTUALLY

REALLY NICE IN REAL LIFE. HAVE YOU MET
HIS PARTNER? SHE'S FROM VENEZUELA!" ANY-
WAY, HE'S ACTUALLY REALLY GREAT! PLEASE
ENJOY   Yeah, yeah
I just really am thinking about so much right now, yeah?
Like, just showers, you know? If I'm happy, if I'm sad, if
I'm hungry, if I'm feeling anything, I shower. And I just
wanted to uplift that.

A VERY SUPPORTIVE PERSON   Oh, absolutely, yeah,
absolutely.
Actually, can I ask everyone here—
I'm a counseling and intervention specialist here on
campus—so, so I want to ask everyone here, as a way
to open up the space and to hold space, please, and just
know this is a safe space—No! This is a brave space! Let's
be brave. I want to ask everyone, what are some things
you like doing in the shower?
For example, I really like to cry in my shower. One time
someone broke up with me, and I forgot he'd left his body
wash in my shower, and I showered with it, and I smelled
him all over me, and I just sat there crying in the shower.
It was so comforting. So now I try to be a shower FOR
other people. So, that's my brave example, is I cry in the
shower. Anyone else?

THE PRESENTER   Well, I uh . . . Sure, I practiced this
presentation in the shower / and—

A VERY SUPPORTIVE PERSON   Wow. Thank you. I
honor that. (*Pivoting to* A VERY TALL EAGER . . .) Do you
want to share something you do in the shower?

A VERY TALL EAGER WHITE MAN THEATER
COLLABORATOR THAT GIVES YOUR THEATER
COMPANY THAT AUTHENTIC "THIS IS A THE-

ATER COMPANY! LOOK AT THIS QUIRKY, VERY
TALL WHITE MAN UP HERE WITH US! MY GOD!
WHAT WILL HE DO!? HE'S GOING TO PLAY A
RACIST IN THIS ONE BUT HE'S ACTUALLY
REALLY NICE IN REAL LIFE. HAVE YOU MET
HIS PARTNER? SHE'S FROM VENEZUELA!" ANY-
WAY, HE'S ACTUALLY REALLY GREAT! PLEASE
ENJOY   Oh, gosh. Um. Yeah, I would love that, actually.
If it's okay for people. Thank you.

A VERY SUPPORTIVE PERSON *is very supportive through
the next monologue.* THE PRESENTER *and* A VERY SMALL
CHILD IN THE AUDIENCE *are still up there, enduring this.
A slide of a gorgeous, upper-middle-class family's glass shower
door appears.*

A VERY TALL EAGER WHITE MAN THEATER
COLLABORATOR THAT GIVES YOUR THEATER
COMPANY THAT AUTHENTIC "THIS IS A THE-
ATER COMPANY! LOOK AT THIS QUIRKY, VERY
TALL WHITE MAN UP HERE WITH US! MY GOD!
WHAT WILL HE DO!? HE'S GOING TO PLAY A
RACIST IN THIS ONE BUT HE'S ACTUALLY
REALLY NICE IN REAL LIFE. HAVE YOU MET
HIS PARTNER? SHE'S FROM VENEZUELA!" ANY-
WAY, HE'S ACTUALLY REALLY GREAT! PLEASE
ENJOY   When I was a kid, I was nine, maybe, we had this
huge, beautiful shower in my parents' house, with gor-
geous glass doors. And I remember I would get in that
shower, and seductively turn it on, and I would play this
game called "Prostitute in the Rain." That's what I would
call it.
I would stand there under the rain, on the street,
Cold and alone, waiting for someone to love me.
My high heels, they hurt so much, so I would press my
hand against the shower door,
pretend it was a car window, and I would beg the men,

Please, please, take me home with you, stud. But these
men,
They would always drive away. And I would just sit there
crying, in the rain.
I've always had this tremendous capacity for empathy
And I think that's why I became an actor.
I think sometimes that the purest way to feel something,
really feel something, is through somebody else. Y'know?

A VERY SUPPORTIVE PERSON   Mmmm, yeah. Yeah,
I completely understand that.
I'm an empath as well. I feel so deeply always. Preferably
through someone else. Sometimes, on my hardest day, I
pretend I'm Julianne Moore in *The Hours*, and the world
just really opens up. Such Clarity. (*To* THE PRESENTER.)
You ever do that?

THE PRESENTER   What? Pretend I'm somebody
else? / No

A VERY SUPPORTIVE PERSON   You should try it. It
really helps you unclench. You seem tight. It'll make you
less tense. With this whole public-speaking thing you seem
to be doing. Do you have any actresses you like? Toni
Colette? Helen Hunt?

THE PRESENTER   Uh . . . I like Laura Linney. She
really seems to have a tremendous amount of certainty.
I'd like that. I really liked her in *Ozark*. And in *Tales of
the City*.

A VERY TALL EAGER WHITE MAN THEATER
COLLABORATOR THAT GIVES YOUR THEATER
COMPANY THAT AUTHENTIC "THIS IS A THE-
ATER COMPANY! LOOK AT THIS QUIRKY, VERY
TALL WHITE MAN UP HERE WITH US! MY GOD!

WHAT WILL HE DO!? HE'S GOING TO PLAY
A RACIST IN THIS ONE BUT HE'S ACTUALLY
REALLY NICE IN REAL LIFE. HAVE YOU MET
HIS PARTNER? SHE'S FROM VENEZUELA!" ANY-
WAY, HE'S ACTUALLY REALLY GREAT! PLEASE
ENJOY   Oh, interesting, interesting! Throwbacks! Mmm,
mmm, mmmhmmm! Thank YOU. Snaps. So, maybe now
if any of you want to ask questions about my process?

A VERY SMALL CHILD IN THE AUDIENCE   Okay,
so would any of you know if it's safe to shower with the
running water since the boil-water notice, or if we should
boil it before bathing with it?

A VERY SUPPORTIVE PERSON   Oh, I'm so sorry. I
see you. You are my other me.

A VERY TALL EAGER WHITE MAN THEATER
COLLABORATOR THAT GIVES YOUR THEATER
COMPANY THAT AUTHENTIC "THIS IS A THE-
ATER COMPANY! LOOK AT THIS QUIRKY, VERY
TALL WHITE MAN UP HERE WITH US! MY GOD!
WHAT WILL HE DO!? HE'S GOING TO PLAY A
RACIST IN THIS ONE BUT HE'S ACTUALLY
REALLY NICE IN REAL LIFE. HAVE YOU MET
HIS PARTNER? SHE'S FROM VENEZUELA!" ANY-
WAY, HE'S ACTUALLY REALLY GREAT! PLEASE
ENJOY   Yeah, that sounds really fuckin' rough, hermano.
My wife is from Venezuela, so I get it. Lo siento.

A VERY SMALL CHILD IN THE AUDIENCE   Thanks,
but I really actually just want to know. I haven't showered
in like three days because I'm / not sure if—

A VERY SUPPORTIVE PERSON   We're actually leading
an accountability workshop in like, an hour, so we gotta
go. But good luck!

The two wraiths exit.

THE PRESENTER   What the fuck is happening?!

A VERY SMALL CHILD IN THE AUDIENCE   You keep conjuring a series of invasive thoughts that manifest in the shape of authority figures and men taking up too much space, effectively rendering all of your anxieties into fractals of your own shame so that you can keep yourself from saying what you actually want to say, probably.

THE PRESENTER   What did you say?

A VERY SMALL CHILD IN THE AUDIENCE   I dunno. Just something my mom used to say.
I'm sorry. I didn't mean to / stop you. Sorry.

THE PRESENTER   (*Nearing his limit.*) Are you done here?! Please! I need to move on, okay?! So, you should / go—

A VERY SMALL CHILD IN THE AUDIENCE   Your hands are shaking. Are you nervous? You're nervous, huh?

THE PRESENTER   (*Disarmed.*) Yes.

A VERY SMALL CHILD IN THE AUDIENCE   Maybe you should hold a pen while you talk.
So you have something to do. I fidget sometimes. If you're ever nervous, it also helps to have a very clear want. Why do you want to keep talking about this stuff if makes you so nervous?
What do you / want?

THE PRESENTER   I want to finish this presentation!!
That's what I want most right now!!! / I feel like you had somewhere to go!

A VERY SMALL CHILD IN THE AUDIENCE You're yelling, so that doesn't seem right, either, / but would you happen to know where I might be able to take a shower?

THE PRESENTER NO! I'M SORRY! I WANT YOU TO GO / AWAY!!

A VERY SMALL CHILD IN THE AUDIENCE *exits.* MX. VASQUEZ *booms.*

LONGTIME PUBLIC-SPEAKING TEACHER MX. VASQUEZ THANK YOU! FINNNAALLY! Good work! Gorgeous! You're doing a fantastic job projecting! Now, stay focused. You cannot let yourself get distracted, kid! Go on!

THE PRESENTER THANK YOU. NEXT SLIDE!

LONGTIME PUBLIC-SPEAKING TEACHER MX. VASQUEZ Breathe.

THE PRESENTER Yes. (*He breathes. A kind of confidence. Curiosity.*) Today, I want to focus on a specific artifact from the annals of the shower's history. I'd like us to turn to the bathhouse. California's earliest bathhouses date back to the gold rush, when entrepreneurs established bathhouses as a way for those manifesting destiny to bathe and sleep after all the murder they were doing.
However, I'd like to attend a less violent history. I'd like to focus on a bathhouse of a different kind.
In preparing for this presentation, I was advised by Mx. Vasquez to tell less and show more.
So we're going to show you. With words. By telling you.

Slide

Slide 8

In this slide, we see the vestiges of the places that were—the defunct Midtowne Spas, the last days of the North Hollywood Spa, the twilight of the Steamworks. Then A PLANT IN THE AUDIENCE, MAYBE AN ACTUAL PLANT, I DON'T KNOW *speaks.*

A PLANT IN THE AUDIENCE, MAYBE AN ACTUAL PLANT, I DON'T KNOW   A bathhouse? What IS That?

THE PRESENTER   Great Question, Rhetorical Device! Some of you may not know what a bathhouse is. And it makes sense that we've forgotten. Many shut down in 1984.
Less than seventy were left in the United States by 2014.
Less than thirty-seven remained open by 2023.
Years later, today, in 2034, after so many, um, political shifts, no bathhouses remain, just their corpses, gutted and repurposed for parking lots, for Paneras, for debtor prisons.
Even schools. This one, for example. Here. Our school.

Yes! The Academy for Innovation and Thought (Go, Einsteins!)—this school was once a bathhouse! A Fun Fact: the custodial closet remains almost entirely intact, and that clock up there, too. In fact, the architecture is still quite similar. The bones of the bathhouse still linger beneath our feet; some pulsing muscle of it is in our walls.

The scars of the building's previous life, waiting to hear its
previous name in a séance.

Once lovingly known as "that shithole near the North
Hollywood Metro Station, not far from Cobra and the
Bullet," all places now closed, this school was once the
North Hollywood Spa!

*The ghost of club music trickles in: trace matter, a portal.
Lights flicker.* THE PRESENTER *is channeling.* WHAT IT
SMELLED LIKE, HOW IT SOUNDED, *and* MAN IN A TOWEL
emerge and prepare the space. Ritual.

WHAT IT SMELLED LIKE   Here's what it smelled like—
Ammonia as in cleaning products, but also piss
Ammonia to clean piss, and piss-poor, and poppers
is what it smelled like, like skin sloughed, and scalp-sweet,
and that yuck-yum, sweat-sweet of rough opened legs,
and bleach, chemical flowers, like cleaned floors dirtied
and dirty floors cleaned!

HOW IT SOUNDED   Here's what it sounded like:
"And I'm to the middle and around again
up to the middle
Up up to the middle and around again
100 percent pure love!"
Room number 45 room number 45 we need your key
room number 45
More Yes No More yes please Oh daddy Oh baby Ow papi
Click Spark Door lock Slap slap slap I'm gonna Oh god
I'm gonna
Key ring key ring key ring huff huff huff THANK YOU.

MAN IN A TOWEL   Here's who was there:
Mostly men, mostly things that look like men
In the darkness, mostly alone, mostly hard-hungry,
Mostly lube-slick, slightly love-sick, mostly stained sheets,

and men in stained towels. I'm a man in a towel.
I'm going to die a little death in here
Not for real die No, too messy. If I die I'll empty myself
and No, I've emptied all my insides to come die here
I flushed water up myself to come here, to be what I want
to be,
Clean Dirty Nasty and Good Oh look: It's a Tuesday
special!
Eight-plus inches get in for free! That's me! Look—

*The cafetorium/classroom this presentation began in looks so
much like what it was once. It's pulsing.*

THE PRESENTER   We are now in the milieu of last,
last, last week.
The North Hollywood Spa. The bathhouse.
These places
Always, somewhere entirely in plain view, somewhere
hidden
Always, someone is coming inside, someone is leaving
Always: steam baths, dry saunas, showers, water, bleach,
wood oil.
Here, through this door, a sling, a hallway of mirrors, a
maze, a hailstorm of hands,
a sliver of light, a glory hole, a cage, a cot, a St. Andrew's
Cross,
a gym nobody is using, a sad vending machine,
and someone next to it is aging and wants.
Don't you want it?
Always these places aging. Longing. Ending.

THE PRESENTER *returns to himself, the dust of flow state still
on him.*

THE PRESENTER   So, in the spirit of less tell and
more show, today, we'll pretend that every place is always
everywhere. That architectures are always haunting each

other across times and geographies. Today, let's imagine
this place as it was once.
This place for beginnings and ends.
Today, let's imagine the grotto, the very bottom floor
of the bathhouse.
The gold-foil numbers on the door of room 32. Here.
Let's imagine.

A club mix of Crystal Waters's "Destination Unknown."
CHELA *enters in her North Hollywood Spa uniform, wheel-
ing her cleaning cart, headphones in. Room 32. She opens the
door. Smoke clouds drift. Someone is there.*

CHELA   Oh. I'm sorry. You're not—are you doing
drugs?

CARLOS   No. (CARLOS *scrambles to hide a little glass pipe
and torch lighter. Their key ring jingles.*) No.

CHELA   You look like you're on drugs.

CARLOS   It's just hot in here.

CHELA   Your eyes look crazy.

CARLOS   No, they don't.

CHELA   Yes, they do. They're too big. What's wrong
with your mouth?

CARLOS   Nothing.

CHELA   Okay, well, you're not supposed to be here. I'm
supposed to clean this room right now. Go home.

CARLOS   I came here with my friends.

CHELA   Go home with them.

CARLOS   I don't know where they are.

Gloria Estefan's "Get on Your Feet" starts playing, inter-rupting Crystal Waters. God, what an awful mix.

CHELA   You want me to call them—we can page them if—if you want me to. It happens a lot. People get lost / here a lot.

CARLOS   They probably left without me!
They weren't my friends.

CHELA   Why'd you come with them then?

CARLOS   I didn't come with them. I came by myself. I just met them here.
They said they wanted to fuck me.

CHELA   Both of them?

CARLOS   Yeah. They're married.

CHELA   Oh? And they're okay with that?

CARLOS   With being married?

CHELA   With having relations with you. In front of each other?

CARLOS   No, they were gonna go at the same time.

CHELA   Go . . . ?

CARLOS   They were gonna fuck me at the same time.
They were gonna DP me.

CHELA   ¡Virgen purísima! Both peepees in your butt?

CARLOS   Yeah.

CHELA   Oh. That's a lot. I get tired even looking at one.

CARLOS   Do you think I can just stay here?

CHELA   No, you gotta go. I'm gonna get in trouble cuz you didn't pay for extra time.

CARLOS   I don't have any money.

CHELA   You can't stay here.

CARLOS   My phone's dead.

CHELA   Charge it.

CARLOS   I don't have a charger.

CHELA   I can lend you mine.

CARLOS   I don't actually have a phone. I lost my stuff.

CHELA   Ay, dios. Muchacho pendejo. Okay, well . . .
. . . You good?

CARLOS   What?

CHELA   What are you chewing?

CARLOS   My cheek.

CHELA   Don't do that. You're gonna bleed.

CARLOS   I'm already bleeding.

CHELA   Oh. Do you want mouthwash?

CARLOS   No, I'm bleeding from my—
In my—

CHELA   Oh. Oh no. Do you need—
You wanna borrow my phone? To call your friends.

CARLOS   I told you, I just met them!! I don't know /
their number!!

CHELA   Who you yelling at, cabrón?!

CARLOS   I'm sorry. I'm just—
Can you—do you think
maybe I can get a ride home with you?

CHELA   Absolutely not.

CARLOS   Please.

CHELA   Where do you live?

CARLOS   To . . . your home?

CHELA   Fuck no.

CARLOS   Will you think about it?

CHELA   I won't.

CARLOS   I don't know where I live right now.
I would be safer in a house with someone who knows
where they live.

CHELA   Ay, chavalo. You're so dumb.
God, you're so young to be this sad and this dumb.

CARLOS   If you don't take me home I'm going to stay here.

CHELA   The manager's gonna call the cops if you stay here!

CARLOS   Then help me.

CHELA   No.

CARLOS   Just tonight. Please. I just need somewhere to be.
If you had a kid . . .
If I was your kid . . .
How would you feel if—

CHELA   I don't got kids.

CARLOS   But if you did.

CHELA   I did. Then I didn't want no kids. So I don't got no kids.
I gotta clean this room. Get up.

CARLOS   I can help. I'll clean this room! Since I made it dirty!
Look, I'll clean it.
I'm cleaning it now.

CHELA   Ay, dios. Fine. Fine! Okay, I will give you a ride home. Not mine. Another home. You can pick. Anywhere between here and Canoga Park, or Van Nuys, or Reseda, or Woodland Hills, or Chatsworth. You would probably like Chatsworth.

CARLOS   Thank you so much! Thank you! You're a life saver! I'm gonna go shower.

(CARLOS *moves toward the door with his stuff*.) And I can
meet you when your shift (CHELA *stops him with a broom*.)
ends.

CHELA   Nah-uh, baby. You can't get something for
nothing, y'know?

CARLOS   But I don't have—

CHELA   You're going to help me, you got it? Between
now and then, you're going to help me clean. We're going
upstairs to get you some clothes.
I have an extra shirt. It's gonna be big. And a hat for you.
Don't talk to nobody and you can't do no sex things again.
You can't make more mess, okay?

CARLOS   I'll try.

CHELA   No. You can't make more mess and if you do,
I'm gonna hit you.
I got a broom and I can punch really hard and I never lost
a fight ever in my life, not even when I fought my cousin,
that fuckin' puta. So you better do what I'm telling you.
What's your name?

CARLOS   Carlos.

CHELA   Okay. You're Sharlie now, okay?

CARLOS   Won't people know I don't work here?

CHELA   Pendejo, nobody cares if anybody works here!
They just want more towels. And lube. Barely.
If anybody asks, just . . .
Just tell them . . .
I don't fuckin' know . . .
You're an intern!

Just no more dicks or butts or nothing, you got it, Sharlie?
Let's go. And grab your shitty sheets, cochino.
I'm Chela, okay? Chela.
Come on!

CHELA *and* CARLOS *exit.*

THE PRESENTER   And they wheel the cleaning cart
out, so you guys exit, okay? Thank you for showing! Great
work! And Chela (that's the woman you saw cleaning)
hates gloves at home, and Carlos (that's the person Chela
found here), they hate condoms here. And Chela thinks,
How will you know your dishes are clean clean if you wear
gloves? How will you know you've killed the germs if your
hands are gloved? But here she wears yellow gloves push-
ing the little yellow cart to clean. The wheels sound like
something dying.
If germs had lungs, if germs were things you could hear
dying, that would be satisfying, yeah?
That's why Carlos hates condoms—they mute all that
good noise. All that living. This is a place to let the skin
feel its living, accompanied. Who wouldn't want to feel together, next to someone else, yeah? Most days, I would like—

*A flow state, club music trickles in again, faint. Lights
flicker. Attuned with the bathhouse, trying to stay on track
with the presentation, but the bathhouse wants to be again.
It wants to exist.*

THE PRESENTER   We are in the milieu of last last last
week, in the mess of the bathhouse. We are in a place of
limbs and skin. A Fact: Fully stretched, human skin is
roughly twenty-two square feet, so imagine all those
bodies next to one another, this canvas of want, stretching
and longing and sagging, all taut and wrinkled and scarred,
all outstretched on a lawn chair, on a bed, on a rubber

sheet. We are now in the deep downstairs. We are with every animal we might be when we are at rest, when we are at want. Here, an echo. A handsome older man rests.

IT HAS BEEN A VERY HARD WEEK *is here, resting.*

IT HAS BEEN A VERY HARD WEEK   I came here to rest.
Here, to age here.
I came here because me and my friends used to come here.

THE PRESENTER   And then, perhaps, one of those Look-but-Don't-Touch Types enters.

LOOK BUT DON'T TOUCH *enters.*

LOOK BUT DON'T TOUCH   I came here to be looked at. But don't touch!
Sometimes, in the dark, hands pop up like flowers
Bouquets of fingers.

IT HAS BEEN A VERY HARD WEEK   That's how Tony Kushner describes the genitals of angels. Bouquets of 'em, of every kind of everything

LOOK BUT DON'T TOUCH   Oh, is that, like, one of your friends?

IT HAS BEEN A VERY HARD WEEK   No.

LOOK BUT DON'T TOUCH   Okay.
. . .
I'm not interested.

IT HAS BEEN A VERY HARD WEEK   I don't want anything you can give me.

LOOK BUT DON'T TOUCH   Why not?

IT HAS BEEN A VERY HARD WEEK   Because you
don't have anything I want.

LOOK BUT DON'T TOUCH   Well, why are you here
then?

IT HAS BEEN A VERY HARD WEEK   Because my
friends used to come here.

LOOK BUT DON'T TOUCH   Okay, but you don't
wanna fuck me?

IT HAS BEEN A VERY HARD WEEK   Do you want to
fuck me?

LOOK BUT DON'T TOUCH   No.

IT HAS BEEN A VERY HARD WEEK   Then I don't. I
just came here to rest.

LOOK BUT DON'T TOUCH   (*Shouts dramatically and
for no good goddamn reason, like a gay banshee.*) Are you
looking at me, you fucking creep?! Are you fucking looking at me? Ugh, this fucking old man is looking! Help! I'm
being groomed!

From under the red cushions, A GHOST UNDER THE RED
CUSHIONS *emerges.*

A GHOST UNDER THE RED CUSHIONS   Oh, shut
up! You're twenty-four, you fucking cum-bucket! Will you
shut the fuck up and just let him rest?!

LOOK BUT DON'T TOUCH *exits, terrified and gay!*

IT HAS BEEN A VERY HARD WEEK   Thank you. It
has been a very hard week.

A GHOST UNDER THE RED CUSHIONS   Yes, it has
been and we miss you very much.

IT HAS BEEN A VERY HARD WEEK   And I miss you
all very much.

A GHOST UNDER THE RED CUSHIONS   Why not
miss us from home?

IT HAS BEEN A VERY HARD WEEK   Because I like
missing you here. I like going missing here. I miss going
here. I'm going missing.
I keep forgetting.
Whenever I start to go missing, I come here and rest and
remember all the things that keep trying to forget
themselves.
It's been such a long time since you were here.

A GHOST UNDER THE RED CUSHIONS   I am
always here.
This is where I was, always, when I met you.
You remember?

IT HAS BEEN A VERY HARD WEEK   I don't. I can't
make out any moment clearly.
But when I sit here, it feels like you, like then.

A GHOST UNDER THE RED CUSHIONS   Then, the
cushions weren't plastic. And we met when you were
already old enough to be the age I was
When I first came here, so I was old enough to have people
to miss already,
which is why I came here.

IT HAS BEEN A VERY HARD WEEK   Yes, that's what
it feels like here.
Like I was always going to be older here. Because you
were. When we met.
You were older here. I was not.

A GHOST UNDER THE RED CUSHIONS   You were
a wild thing with open legs and hungry arms
And every time you smiled with open legs, I swear, you
looked like you'd won.

IT HAS BEEN A VERY HARD WEEK   I was younger
then, so I was always winning.

A GHOST UNDER THE RED CUSHIONS   I was
older then, so I always let you win.
I've been gone for a shorter time than I was alive.
So I'm younger now, than I was then.

IT HAS BEEN A VERY HARD WEEK   And me? I am
older now?

A GHOST UNDER THE RED CUSHIONS   Than me?
Yes, you are older now. Here.

IT HAS BEEN A VERY HARD WEEK   Is there anywhere I am not?

A GHOST UNDER THE RED CUSHIONS   Older?
Yes. Back then you aren't.
Someday you won't be at all.

IT HAS BEEN A VERY HARD WEEK   Someday I
won't be older at all.

A GHOST UNDER THE RED CUSHIONS   No,
someday you won't be at all.

IT HAS BEEN A VERY HARD WEEK   Oh. Someday I
won't be.

A GHOST UNDER THE RED CUSHIONS   The same
way I am not.
But by then, the time between us, it'll make you a boy
again.

IT HAS BEEN A VERY HARD WEEK   And that will
make you a very young daddy.

A GHOST UNDER THE RED CUSHIONS   The math
all does itself. So, tell me, if you can't remember, what
does it feel like?

IT HAS BEEN A VERY HARD WEEK   Like you're
lying next to me, and like the good poppers. The kind
that would make you go blind if you did too much.
And like when you'd laugh at me like I didn't know any
better.
I didn't know any better.

A GHOST UNDER THE RED CUSHIONS   And I'd
say, "It's not like it was here anymore. Back when I first
started coming here, I tell you, we didn't have rights, but
we really used to fuck! We used to do everything here.
And there was a lady sometimes. She would sing right
over there."

IT HAS BEEN A VERY HARD WEEK   And I would
listen to you.

A GHOST UNDER THE RED CUSHIONS   You
wouldn't. You were a very bad listener.
You were just watching for your turn in the conversation.

IT HAS BEEN A VERY HARD WEEK   I was waiting for
you to breed me. I just wanted you to want me.

A GHOST UNDER THE RED CUSHIONS   Sweet kid.
Very stupid.

IT HAS BEEN A VERY HARD WEEK   I never got any
smarter.

A GHOST UNDER THE RED CUSHIONS   You never
got any stupider.
That counts for something.

IT HAS BEEN A VERY HARD WEEK   When did I get
older here, you think?

A GHOST UNDER THE RED CUSHIONS   Sometime
yesterday, probably.

IT HAS BEEN A VERY HARD WEEK   Do you remember much more? I am trying very hard and I just keep
getting lost.

A GHOST UNDER THE RED CUSHIONS   Are you
trying to remember me or you?

IT HAS BEEN A VERY HARD WEEK   Both of us. I
miss you.
I miss myself with you.
Every time I try to remember, I go missing all over the
hallways here.
Sometimes I go missing in the hot tub.
We met there, yes?

A GHOST UNDER THE RED CUSHIONS   You
remember!

We miss you, too. All of us in the cracks too hard to scrub.
All of us still here, caked in the cracks, we miss you, too.

IT HAS BEEN A VERY HARD WEEK   One day, will I
be there?

A GHOST UNDER THE RED CUSHIONS   In the
cracks? Oh, yes. One day, you will be here so hard you'll
be almost impossible to scrub off. And one day, this spot
is going to feel like you so much, you'll be hard to miss.

IT HAS BEEN A VERY HARD WEEK   Where is
everyone else?

All these GHOSTS *emerge.*

A GHOST UNDER THE STAIRS   Here.

A GHOST BEHIND THE DOOR   And here.

A GHOST BEHIND THE CLOCK   And here.

A PARTY OF GHOSTS! WITH THEIR LIMBS
SPRAWLED ALL OVER THE PLACE, THEY ARE
SO HAPPY TO SEE YOU!   We are so happy to see you
here, with our limbs sprawled all over the place! We miss
you so much!

IT HAS BEEN A VERY HARD WEEK   I miss you all
too. Thank you.

A VERY REAL TWINK *enters.*

A VERY REAL TWINK   Hey.

IT HAS BEEN A VERY HARD WEEK   Hey there.

A VERY REAL TWINK   You here by yourself?

IT HAS BEEN A VERY HARD WEEK   Yes.

A PARTY OF GHOSTS! WITH THEIR LIMBS
SPRAWLED ALL OVER THE PLACE, THEY ARE
SO HAPPY TO SEE YOU!   Oooooooooh!

A VERY REAL TWINK   I'm not bothering you, am I?
If I just lie here next to you?

IT HAS BEEN A VERY HARD WEEK   People usually
don't talk in these kinds of places.

A VERY REAL TWINK   Oh, I'm sorry.

IT HAS BEEN A VERY HARD WEEK   No, don't be.
It's nice to talk to someone nice.

A PARTY OF GHOSTS! WITH THEIR LIMBS
SPRAWLED ALL OVER THE PLACE, THEY ARE
SO HAPPY TO SEE YOU!   Ooooooh!

A VERY REAL TWINK   (*He reaches for* IT HAS BEEN A
VERY HARD WEEK*'s body.*)
May I—

IT HAS BEEN A VERY HARD WEEK   Sure. Are you
okay if I—

A VERY REAL TWINK   Please. Do.

A PARTY OF GHOSTS! WITH THEIR LIMBS
SPRAWLED ALL OVER THE PLACE, THEY ARE
SO HAPPY TO SEE YOU!   You're not supposed to
ask. You just do.

IT HAS BEEN A VERY HARD WEEK   I like the
talking. The asking. I think it's sweet.

A VERY REAL TWINK   What?

IT HAS BEEN A VERY HARD WEEK   Oh, not you.
Sorry.

A PARTY OF GHOSTS! WITH THEIR LIMBS
SPRAWLED ALL OVER THE PLACE, THEY ARE
SO HAPPY TO SEE YOU!   And now!

IT HAS BEEN A VERY HARD WEEK *and* A VERY REAL
TWINK *are too close now, the* GHOSTS *returning a bit more
clearly at the sight of this possibility. The lights flicker, then
dim.*

THE PRESENTER   (*He commands it, his own stunted
desire.*) Here it is too dark to clearly see the details of what
they are doing, maybe only the outlines of want. So it's
best if we just imagine your favorite time in the dark,
naked, with someone who made you feel like you weren't
missing.
Just imagine. That is the extent of desire sometimes, no?
The impossibly thick border between want and the actual
thing wanted. So, we imagine.

And now imagine THE PRESENTER *swirling, up, down into
another world's version of himself, jealous, flustered. Angry
horny? The lights of the cafetorium/classroom start to leak
back like molasses.*

THE PRESENTER   For example, I imagine the attendants at the bathhouses. I imagine often what it must be
like, to be a stationary person behind a cash register, in
front of a wall of keys, a rack of flip-flops and Rhino boner

pills. How frustrating, to usher in everyone's wants and see so little of them. To be reminded nightly of all the things you might want, and do much less than that. How painful to be a disembodied voice while other people get to be bodies, get to be touched. I imagine the attendants painfully in their tiny booths, waiting to interrupt / touch—

LONGTIME PUBLIC-SPEAKING TEACHER MX. VASQUEZ   Hold. You're telling us again. You were doing so great showing. Show us what you mean. What did these attendants sound like?

THE PRESENTER   Oh, sure. (*Then his* ATTENDANT *voice emerges; a wall of key rings and receipts, and a microphone manifest!*) "Locker 74, please come turn in your key, please! Locker 74, your time is up. Please. Thank you."

The GHOSTS *disappear.* A VERY REAL TWINK *and* IT HAS BEEN A VERY HARD WEEK *do too.* THE PRESENTER *watches them go. The ugly, charter school cafetorium/classroom lights return.*

THE PRESENTER   Wow. Um. More on them later, maybe, but there may not be time.
There may just be a Google form at the end of this.
Feedback for the department.
So make sure you fill out that Google form!

LONGTIME PUBLIC-SPEAKING TEACHER MX. VASQUEZ   Oh, come on!

THE PRESENTER   (*A panic button!*) Slide!

Slide

Slide 9

Technical difficulties. Word clouds. Fuck.

THE PRESENTER (*A pause. Hunger lingering.*) So
sorry, everyone. We actually . . .
Okay, so, oh—wait—sorry.

LONGTIME PUBLIC-SPEAKING TEACHER MX.
VASQUEZ You shouldn't apologize to / your audience.

THE PRESENTER Riiiiiight! Fuck—oop—fudge! Wait.
I lost my place.
Oh god.
I lost my place
Uh—

JUST HAPPY TO HELP! ARE YOU OKAY? *comes to the rescue.*

JUST HAPPY TO HELP! ARE YOU OKAY? Hi,
everyone! I'm just going to do some free word association
here. I'm going to say some words, and you're going to
just respond back with whatever word pops into your
head!
Just to—
So it feels less—
Just to feel less! Okay, here we go!!
Water (*Wait for one-word response, then no matter what it is
say this next word anyway.*)

Steam. (*Same as above. We are going to follow a pattern and I'm not going to write this again.*)

Wet.

Shower.

Shoreline.

Charcuterie.

Gymnos.

THE PRESENTER   Gym! Yes, gym! Okay, we're no longer playing word association.
I don't like it very much, but audience interaction is important in presentations.

LONGTIME PUBLIC-SPEAKING TEACHER MX. VASQUEZ   Nice work! Collaboration! Audience participation AND good recovery?! It's like *The King's Speech* in here! What a movie! Now, /can you get back—

THE PRESENTER   YES! SO, GYMNOS is the Greek word for naked. So, "gymnasium" is like the Greek way of saying to train naked, and where do we spend most of our naked time? IN THE SHOWER! Unless you don't shower and spend more time naked elsewhere. I'm not judging. At any rate, what are we training for in there?! Is the shower a gym? Is the rectum a grave? Is the mother a place? I argue that the shower is a place where we train, a place to have difficult conversations, to write a new thing, to process grief, to practice attuning ourselves to all the smells we make, to temper all the smells we made, to train ourselves to think of smells as evidence to be hidden! To not use shampoo or liquid soap from the school bathroom as lubricant! / To—

JUST HAPPY TO HELP! ARE YOU OKAY?   Oh god,
that's just awful.

THE PRESENTER   Yes, it is.

JUST HAPPY TO HELP! ARE YOU OKAY?   Did that
happen to you?

THE PRESENTER   Yes. Yes, it did.

JUST HAPPY TO HELP! ARE YOU OKAY?   Well, what
happened?

THE PRESENTER   Oh. Um. Well, well, I was I was on
campus and um, I was in the restroom and I was washing
my hands. And this guy I had this huge crush on in my
English class, he um—
Yeah, he walks in and he sees me and I guess, I dunno. He
just sees me
He sees me and he asks if I wanted to—
Well, no,
Well, he said he wanted to fuck me, um, and I, I really
liked him a lot. I'd look at his hands sometimes and just
think about his fingers in class randomly. What his palms
might feel like.
So I figured. I dunno. I just really wanted him to like me
and,
And he was there in the bathroom and I was there
and he closes the door. I try to kiss him but
But he doesn't kiss me and
And, uh
I didn't know you could use spit as lube
so he just sort of reached for the hand soap dispenser
and, yeah, he used the soap to—

JUST HAPPY TO HELP! ARE YOU OKAY?   Goodness
gracious! That's not supposed to go in there.

THE PRESENTER   I know.

JUST HAPPY TO HELP! ARE YOU OKAY?   Well, what
did you do?

THE PRESENTER   I let him finish.

JUST HAPPY TO HELP! ARE YOU OKAY?   Oh. And?

THE PRESENTER   And it hurt a lot. It burned. And
Hehe uh then, uh, haha ugh
then I saw him in class that afternoon and
He wouldn't look at me at all. He wouldn't look
And I just sat there at my tiny desk, burning.

JUST HAPPY TO HELP! ARE YOU OKAY?   Oh, you
poor thing. That must have been awful.

THE PRESENTER   I mean, sort of. But whatever. Well,
okay, maybe this is just me, but the burning sort of made
me feel like maybe I was now cleaner than I started out.
It was terrible and that made me feel like maybe it was
working. The soap. I felt cleaner inside all day, while I
burned. And I felt clear. About us. And me and him. That's
when you feel cleanest, and clear about how things work—
when it's painful. Yes, that's the thing I think I'm trying to
get at! Yes! Cleanliness is difficult, painful even! Cleanliness
requires discomfort! Disinfection requires arduous scrubbing and chemicals and should be done until the dirty
thing is clean! / Bathhouses are a—

JUST HAPPY TO HELP! ARE YOU OKAY?   I . . . I
don't think that's a very healthy approach to cleanliness at
all. Or boys, / like, at all.

THE PRESENTER   And that's why this isn't a question
and answer period!

That's why this is still a presentation, and nobody asked
you to open your mouth. Okay!
Now where were we?

JUST HAPPY TO HELP! ARE YOU OKAY?   Asshole.

JUST HAPPY TO HELP! ARE YOU OKAY? *exits.*

THE PRESENTER   I'd like us to return to the broader
topic of cleanliness now, to just, yeah—
It might feel less—Yes!
Bathing provides an / opportunity—

From the audience A CONQUISTADOR! WITH ONE OF
THOSE HATS! *interrupts.*

A CONQUISTADOR! WITH ONE OF THOSE
HATS!   This bath. Why?

THE PRESENTER   I'm sorry?

A CONQUISTADOR! WITH ONE OF THOSE
HATS!   Why do you bath?

THE PRESENTER   Bathe?

A CONQUISTADOR! WITH ONE OF THOSE
HATS!   You will not speak to me this way!

THE PRESENTER   Um, did we . . . who let this man in?

A CONQUISTADOR! WITH ONE OF THOSE
HATS!   I AM HERE ON A MISSION FROM GOD
AND I NEED NO PERMISSION BUT DIVINITY TO
OPEN THE WAY TO ANY LAND I SEE FIT! I AM
THE ONE WHO RIDES THROUGH GROUNDS
DANGEROUS AND UKNOWN! I AM FRANCISCO

GAMEZ LOPEZ DE GAMA MÁRQUEZ FERNANDEZ
DEL TORO VILLACRUZ AND I AM SENT HERE
BY THE VERY SAME FORCES THAT COMPEL
THE STORM AND THE RAIN! I WILL NOT BE
QUESTIONED!

THE PRESENTER   Okay, but did you register through
Eventbrite, though, or did someone just send you the
invitation directly? This cafetorium is pretty hard to find /
and I don't remember letting you in—

A CONQUISTADOR! WITH ONE OF THOSE
HATS!   YOU WILL ANSWER MY QUERY!
WHY DO YOU BATH!?

THE PRESENTER   (*He approaches* A CONQUISTADOR!
. . . *Then:*) Alright, sir, that's—Oh-wow—Oh—oooof—
You—That smell is—
How did we not catch this?
Oh god. Ugh—(*Retching.*)

A CONQUISTADOR! WITH ONE OF THOSE
HATS!   Hey, that's not nice.

THE PRESENTER   Christ! Are you dead?! This is like,
Somebody shit inside a bag of parmesan and baked it
inside a corpse in some hideous oven powered by burning
hair and the oven is in a sewer and even then
My god!

A CONQUISTADOR! WITH ONE OF THOSE
HATS!   Hey! (*He starts to weep.*) That's not very nice at
all! You stop that! You stop that right now! (*Weeping!*)

THE PRESENTER   Are you . . . are you crying? Oh no,
not the little conquistador crying?

Aww, little shitty-diaper baby conquistador got his feelings
hurt?
Aww, pobrecito, chiquito! I think
I think now is a really great time
To imagine. Yes. To play. Let's play!
WASH! THAT! FUCKER!
SLIDE, PLEASE!

Slide

Slide 10

*It's a game! It's a show! We're playing now! A sign flashes
"Applause!" or maybe a random in a banana hammock
comes onstage with a cardboard sign reading the same. It's
a colonial revenge fantasy! It's impossible!*

THE PRESENTER   We're role-playing now! We're doing
this in the space of play, okay, so there's no scary identity
breaks! It's like Kahoot! This is part of the thing, you guys,
okay!?! WHO WANTS MORE SHOWING?! Yeah! So,
FRANCISCO GAMEZ LOPEZ DE GAMA MÁRQUEZ
FERNANDEZ DEL TORO VILLACRUZ!

*A sign flashes "Boo this fucker!" or just another sexy person in
a thong holds up some posterboard.*

THE PRESENTER   Francisco, you'll be playing the floor
of a very dirty private room in a bathhouse. Are you up for
the challenge?

A CONQUISTADOR! WITH ONE OF THOSE
HATS!   Please, don't—

THE PRESENTER   TOO FUCKING BAD!
WOOOOOOOOO!!!!!!!

A CONQUISTADOR! WITH ONE OF THOSE
HATS!   NO!!!!!!!!!!!!!!

THE PRESENTER   (*A dom.*) Get on the floor.
You're now the very dirty floor of a very dirty private room
in a bathhouse. Got it.
(*A boxing match!*) And now, all the way from Canoga
Park, she's five seven, she's Mexican American and kinda
mean, but at least she's got a car now! It's her fourth day
on Herbalife shakes and She! Is! Tired! Straight from the
Saturday night shift at the North Hollywood Spa! Here's
CHELA!

CHELA *enters with her cart, her lunch bag slung over her
shoulder. Another sign flashes. "Silence is complicity. Cheer
for Chela!"—if posterboard, then the sexy person flashes this
and exits.*

A CONQUISTADOR! WITH ONE OF THOSE
HATS!   Please, no. I am unsuitable to be a floor! / Please

THE PRESENTER   GET DOWN THERE, PIG! We'll
imagine I'm an attendant, so I am an attendant. Which
sometimes means I'm the manager, which means I call the
shots, so I call the shots!
So, I'm daddy and not baby.
(THE PRESENTER'S ATTENDANT *voice emerges.*) "Chela, We
need room 76 clean, please.
Room 76 needs cleaning.
Thank you, hon."

CHELA   Goddamn it! I can't even fucking eat here. Can't
even sit down in peace.
One day I'm going to sit down and I'm going to eat a
sandwich right here.
After I clean it, one of these days, I'm really gonna take a
goddamn break.

THE PRESENTER   "Room 76 needs cleaning, please!"

CHELA   Pinche puto. One of these days I'm going to eat
this sandwich and I'm gonna take off my bra and let my
tits breathe, right here, and I'm gonna put my feet in some
warm / water—

THE PRESENTER   "Chela! Room 76, please! Now!"

CHELA   There's not going to be no dirty floors one day.
Just Epsom salts and lotions.
I'm going to have my hair down one day.
Wear pretty earrings, pearls maybe, and put cucumbers
over my eyes.
But then I'll eat one, like in the movies.
And then someone will come and wrap my legs in plastic
so they'll be pretty.
I'm gonna smell like mint and money.
Maybe someone will paint my toenails a cute color. A
tangerine.
I can't wait to sit down one day. Right here.

THE CONQUISTADOR, NOW PLAYING THE
FLOOR   (*Empathy.*) Okay, but I kind of see this for her.
She is tired. / I think I understand what—

THE PRESENTER   "CHELA, We really need you to do
your job, please! So, room 76 needs cleaning!"

CHELA   YES! Pivot.
I will clean this place.
I will wheel my cart to clean this place.
The placid water, and the skin in it, the hair in it, the cum
in it.
I will wheel my cart to clean the crap out of this place.
I will wheel my war and will through this place and I will
win

I will win my war of dirt and bleach and sickness and steam
And here is how I will win.

THE CONQUISTADOR, NOW PLAYING THE FLOOR   PLEASE, / DON'T!

CHELA   (*She scrubs with spite. With murder.*) And a floor can't speak, a floor can't feel things.
But I can, in this room, alone, I can speak and I can feel,
So I will say, "God, it smells like fucking shit in here. Disgusting!"

THE CONQUISTADOR, NOW PLAYING THE FLOOR   MY BACK! OH GOD!

CHELA   And the floor can't feel my feet, but I can smell the dirty, dirty floor
So, I'll scrub it hard, hot water clean. Hot, bleach, clean!
I'll imagine the germs screaming in every voice that ever called me dirty! In all their oldest names
and every uniform they ever wore when they called us that! Dirty!
That's how good I clean. / Until the floor screams!

THE CONQUISTADOR, NOW PLAYING THE FLOOR   Oh god, it hurts so much to be the floor!
OH CHRIST! ¡DIOS, OS ROGÁIS, ESCUCHA / MI PLEGARIA!

CHELA   And a floor is not allowed to speak
Or have a god that isn't me!
If the floor had skin it would break.
I'm that good at this. I'm that good at getting things clean,

which is why I don't have kids, because I'd clean them till they burst, and all kids ever do is get dirty, is make mess.
So I never had no kids!
Carlos!
Come here, kid!

CARLOS *enters.*

CARLOS   Yeah—Oh god
It smells here.

CHELA   Ay, no seas mamón. It wasn't all roses in the room I found you in, marrano.
Bring me the Clorox from the little room. And get gloves.

CARLOS   For what?

CHELA   You're going to help me clean this room.

CARLOS   Okay.

CHELA   You say, "Yes, ma'am."

CARLOS   Yes, ma'am-

CHELA   Good boy. Go.

CARLOS *exits.*

CHELA   Yes. (CHELA *scrubs* THE CONQUISTADOR, NOW PLAYING THE FLOOR *hard. Murder. Fury. A general.*) I clean very, very good.
I clean here for the boys, so the boys are safe
Because the boys are crazy.
Ay, no, crazy, crazy boys with crazy eyes and their little red shorts

And the red walls, years and years of red walls and red
shorts, and red eyes, and red holes
Red crazy boys
Red everywhere.
So crazy, those boys.
Ay no. So sweet sometimes, so sweet.
But they make things so, so dirty.
So dirty sometimes. Don't say hi sometimes. Sometimes
don't say hi never. So rude.
"Pass by quickly, Chela! Quickly please, Chela!
You'll scare the customers. If they see you, you'll scare
them, Chela!
Get in and clean quick."
Like shit and blood don't take time, don't take a hard heart
to clean, don't take a hard hand and a hard stare
to leave myself while I clean all that red and brown,
all that smell and skin, but I'm good. I'm that good
and I'm that quick, on my hands and knees and legs,
I'm that good at leaving things clean, leaving myself
I'm
That
Good!

God.

CARLOS *enters.*

CARLOS   I brought the Clorox.

CHELA   Throw a little cap—
No. Three caps in that water right there.
You're going to mop the floor.

CARLOS   How do you mop stuff?

CHELA   What do you mean?

CARLOS   I don't know how.
My mom said I wouldn't be good at it.
So I never did it.

CHELA   You're a shit son and a worse intern.
Take the mop, and the bleach water, and run it on the
floor.
Put your weight on it. Like you're mad at yourself.

CARLOS   Like this?

CHELA   Yes, just like that, but sadder. Yeah, that's
good.
This is you paying me back, okay?
For making that other room dirty.

CARLOS   I'm sorry I made a mess.

CHELA   Ya, pinche mitotero.
Shut up. You like mess. It's okay to like mess. It's fun.

CARLOS   Really? You think it's okay / to—

CHELA   ¡Ey, puto! I didn't say stop mopping!
Okay, okay, that's good.
That's how you mop. Nice.

CARLOS   And what are you going to do?

CHELA   I'm gonna . . .
I'm gonna supervise you. I'm your supervisor now.
"That's really good, Sharlie! Good job!"

CARLOS   "Wow! Thank you, boss! Do you think
someday I could get a promotion?"
Is that what I'm supposed to say back?

CHELA   Yeah, that's pretty good. Except don't ask for nothing.
You never get nothing here. So you just do your job good y ya.

CARLOS   "Wow! Thank you, boss! Thank you for this job!"

CHELA   Yeah, that's good. (*She pulls out a gorgeous lipstick color and applies it to her lips.*) What do you think, Sharlie?

CARLOS   Werq.

CHELA   What?

CARLOS   It's nice. (*He winces. His hole.*)

CHELA   Sharlie, is your butt okay?

CARLOS   Oh, yeah. Yeah, I'm good. I think.
Just a fissure probably.

CHELA   A fisher? What do you mean?

CARLOS   Oh, like a cut on my hole.

CHELA   Don't say it like that. Say "butt."
So, like a hemorrhoid?

CARLOS   No. Like a tear.

CHELA   Ay, qué feo. Okay, I think that floor looks pretty good.

THE CONQUISTADOR WHO WAS THE FLOOR,
NOW STANDING BY THE DOOR   I think this floor

looks fucking great. (THE CONQUISTADOR *vapes*.) Wooo,
Shit. God, I feel . . . I feel new. Mmm. That's good work.
Strong backs and shoulders. Look at you both. Wearing all
that shoulder out to get me good and clean!

CHELA   Yeah, give it an hour. It'll end up just as shitty
as we found it. I hate it here.

THE CONQUISTADOR WHO WAS THE FLOOR,
NOW STANDING BY THE DOOR   FUCK! I'm so
fucking horny now! I will leave this scene and fuck everything in another one!
For the sake of allegory. In a different costume. But with
the same ethic of rigidity and control!
Here I go. Footstep footstep footstep.

THE CONQUISTADOR WHO WAS THE FLOOR, NOW
STANDING BY THE DOOR *exits.*

THE PRESENTER   Okay, that was great, guys. But wait
a minute, you might be saying,
What does this have to do with cleanliness? I thought /
this was about bath—

CHELA   Sharlie, take the sheets and the pillowcases and
bring me clean ones. We gotta do the VIP rooms after.
And then the downstairs.

CARLOS   Yes, ma'am.

THE PRESENTER   Uh, guys. We're good. As I was
saying, / you might be—

CARLOS   (*To* CHELA.) Hey. Do you think if I—
If I do a really good job, like I just did,
do you think I could fuck for a little bit?

I didn't get a chance to cum.
I promise I won't get anything on anything else.

CHELA   No!

THE PRESENTER   . . . Uh, guys? Can we—Anyway,
you, uh, you might be thinking, "Oh, I thought this was
about bathhouses and cleanliness. What does this have to
do with colonialism?" As I mentioned earlier, / racialized
notions of—

CHELA (*To* CARLOS.)   Oye, y luego, go see if anybody is
in the little hammock.

CARLOS   The sling?

CHELA   Andale, esa madre.

THE PRESENTER   Guys!!

CARLOS   What if someone's using it?

CHELA   Tell them they got ten minutes. That we gotta
let the room breathe. Put the "closed for maintenance"
sign up. I don't wanna clean that shit again.

THE PRESENTER   GUYS!? (*Dialing into his* ATTEN-
DANT *voice.*) "We need custodial in the lounge, please.
Custodial, we need you to tidy up the lounge."

CHELA   Ugh, come on, Sharlie. They're calling you.

CARLOS *and* CHELA *exit.*

THE PRESENTER   "Thank you, huns!" Anyway, I
would like to return to our earlier discussion and highlight

the ways in which racialized notions of cleanliness and
sexist forms of desire have contributed to the demise of
bathhouses, exacerbated by the various pandemics we've
endured over the years. / Here, I would also argue—

THE CDC *from offstage.*

THE CDC   UH OH! Did I hear the r-word AND the
p-word?! NOPE NOPE NOPE!
Slide!

THE CDC *enters and forcefully moves* THE PRESENTER *into
a seat.*

Slide

Slide 11

And now, state-sanctioned smut! With Laura Linney!

THE CDC   HI THERE! CDC here. Kids these days,
huh? (*To* THE PRESENTER, *saccharine and cruel.*) What a
precocious little pig you are! Here's a Dum-Dum! (*To the
audience, PR crisis management.*) Just here to make sure
that we're not spreading any misinformation here!
So, I'd like to do that by changing the subject!
I get asked a lot, "What's it like, being the Centers for
Disease Control?"
And I'll tell you, it isn't easy. Diseases don't follow the
rules! They rule the night!
Now yes, admittedly, we're currently in another p-word;
you know what I'm talking about. (THE CDC *sprays Febreze
in the air.*) Anyway, given the current p-word, we really
recommend that if you MUST intercourse, if you absolutely haaave to intercourse, we recommend um . . . well
we aren't discouraging the Exclusive use of Glory Holes
at this time.
Here, we've brought Laura Linney to explain.

LAURA LINNEY, BROUGHT TO YOU BY THE CDC! *enters.*

LAURA LINNEY, BROUGHT TO YOU BY THE
CDC!   Hi, I'm Golden Globe Award winner and coping
mechanism Laura Linney! You might remember me from
my stunning turn as a white woman on the brink of

emotional collapse, but with a great deal of certainty and authority!

THE PRESENTER   (*Starstruck!*) No fuckin' way!?

LAURA LINNEY, BROUGHT TO YOU BY THE
CDC!   (*With absolute grace.*) Yes fuckin' way.
Tonight, I'd like to talk to you about Glory Holes. A Glory Hole is a hole to present the genitals for oral, digital, or penetrative stimulation. This is key in a pand—

THE CDC   Nope. We can say p-word. Or Panera.

LAURA LINNEY, BROUGHT TO YOU BY THE
CDC!   Thank you. In a pa . . . Panera, it's important to avoid the spread of particles that may carry disease such as . . . Co . . uh, Monk . . . nope . . . other things. Like . . . mumps?

THE CDC   Good. Yeah, if you name any disease post-'82, we might alienate our voter base, so, maybe just—

LAURA LINNEY, BROUGHT TO YOU BY THE
CDC!   Do we maybe have another word that we can—

THE CDC   Skip to the tutorial. We can only afford you for like two more minutes.

LAURA LINNEY, BROUGHT TO YOU BY THE
CDC!   Thank you.
Find a wall somewhere near you, or put up a strong, plastic shower curtain at a threshold in your home, or maybe go to the restroom of a liberal arts building of a college in Texas and just put a hole in that barrier, big enough to present your goodies. Your cookies. Your jewels.
Once the hole is there, you never have to look at anyone.

Sometimes, I pretend it's just a younger version of myself
on the other end, because then it's masturbation. Mutual
masturbation, but with yourself, but it's another person!
And voilà!
Glory!
Am I done here? Who do I give my W-9 to?

THE CDC   Just email that to me as a signed PDF. I can
forward that to the school.

LAURA LINNEY, BROUGHT TO YOU BY THE
CDC!   Fantastic.

THE PRESENTER   Wow. Uh. Thank you, Miss Linney.
Huge fan!

LAURA LINNEY, BROUGHT TO YOU BY THE
CDC!   Thank you. I'm playing a homo's sister again next
month, so this feels right. I'm gonna go do Meisner in the
porno room.
I'm Laura Linney.
I'm Laura Linney.

LAURA LINNEY, BROUGHT TO YOU BY THE CDC! *exits.*

THE CDC   Wow! Yes. You can certainly tell she was in
Tales of the City! Am I right?
Armistead Maupin?! I don't even know her!
God, I wish I was dead.
So yeah, again, we just wanted to make sure we cover some
basics given the horny topic at hand in this presentation.
So, with all the bathhouses closed down, please remember:
so long as you're in a p-word, maybe just carry some ply-
wood around with a hole in it, put some handles or a
harness on it!
Like a GoPro Glory Hole! GoProHole! Gophers!

My god, this is exhausting.
Is this thing almost over?

A VERY SMALL CHILD IN THE AUDIENCE *returns.*

A VERY SMALL CHILD IN THE AUDIENCE   Hi.
This is all very informative. But / I still

THE PRESENTER   Oh god. No, kid, I told / you—

A VERY SMALL CHILD IN THE AUDIENCE   just
wanted to know about the boil-water notice in my city.
There's been so many slides since we last talked about this
and it's been a few months and we still don't have potable
water.

THE CDC   Potable?

A VERY SMALL CHILD IN THE AUDIENCE   Oh,
water you can drink. It's the same word in Spanish and
English. I learned that just a few weeks ago.
When we stopped having potable water.
I want to know if we should boil the water we shower
with. I tried showering, and I got this rash / and—

THE CDC   Look, most of that information was just
Linney winging it. That's how it works around here, okay?
We get presented a prompt, or a problem, or a presentation, and we just sorta wing it, and things eventually work
themselves out, okay? We are so understaffed and we're
barely scraping by as a credible agency after all the p-words,
so we just come to this kind of shit for the community
engagement.
Your guess is as good as mine, kid.
Here. Have this small bottle of hand sanitizer.
Maybe someone can help you in the next section of this
thing.

THE CDC *runs away.*

A VERY SMALL CHILD IN THE AUDIENCE   Do you think we can figure out what the next section is about? I really mostly just want somewhere to shower.

THE PRESENTER   Uh . . . yes. Yes, that is . . . That is a fantastic transition! Thank fuck, some structure! Yes!

A VERY SMALL CHILD IN THE AUDIENCE   So, you do know where I can shower?

THE PRESENTER   Yes. Next slide, please!

Slide

Slide 12

THE PRESENTER   We are in the milieu of last last last last last week. At the bathhouse. At the North Hollywood Spa.

THE PRESENTER's ATTENDANT *voice emerges again. The classroom walls tremble with the bathhouse past, a summoning. A locker room area blooms. The shower area and toilets spring forth, too.*

THE PRESENTER   Sometime, in another world, I greet you at the door, and I say "Do you have a membership with us?" And you'll say

A VERY SMALL CHILD IN THE AUDIENCE   "No."

THE PRESENTER   And I won't even look at you. "Locker or room?" I'll say, and resent you.

A VERY SMALL CHILD IN THE AUDIENCE "Locker,"

THE PRESENTER   you'll say, and I'll say "It's $35 for a locker if you're not a member." And you'll hand me a card, and I'll buzz you in and hand you a towel.
Envious, I'll watch you go inside the locker room area.
Jingling key rings everywhere and bouquets of dicks.
You're not concerned with any of that. You have a copy of *Howards End* in your book bag. Ugh. What the fuck is

82

that about? Anyway, you just want somewhere to shower, but you haven't showered in four days, and if you took your clothes off in front of all these people, they'd sniff you out. What to do?

A VERY SMALL CHILD IN THE AUDIENCE *enters the bathhouse. Then a man enters:* A COCK GOBLIN, ONE OF HIS BALLS IS ABNORMALLY LARGER THAN THE OTHER.

A VERY SMALL CHILD IN THE AUDIENCE   Hi, uh, excuse me. I saw that this was a bathhouse.

A COCK GOBLIN, ONE OF HIS BALLS IS ABNOR-MALLY LARGER THAN THE OTHER   Your first time here?

A VERY SMALL CHILD IN THE AUDIENCE   Yeah, I just wanted to know if I could shower here. My city just issued a boil-water notice—

A COCK GOBLIN, ONE OF HIS BALLS IS ABNOR-MALLY LARGER THAN THE OTHER   You like to suck dick?

A VERY SMALL CHILD IN THE AUDIENCE   That's a really weird question, given my character's name.

A COCK GOBLIN, ONE OF HIS BALLS IS ABNOR-MALLY LARGER THAN THE OTHER   Oh, I apolo-gize. It's just, you're actually a whole-ass adult right now, so I just figured—

A VERY SMALL CHILD IN THE AUDIENCE   Oh.

A VERY SMALL CHILD IN THE AUDIENCE *undresses and becomes* A WHOLE-ASS ADULT, *waiting to shower.*

A WHOLE-ASS ADULT   Oh, I see it now. I forgot. No
thanks on the dick, though.

A COCK GOBLIN, ONE OF HIS BALLS IS ABNOR-
MALLY LARGER THAN THE OTHER   Your loss.
Anyway, there's showers over there, right around the
corner. Just put your clothes in your locker and you can
shower.
Hey, before you go,
can you suck it a little?

A WHOLE-ASS ADULT   Thank you. Uh. No, I—I
don't think so.

A COCK GOBLIN, ONE OF HIS BALLS IS ABNOR-
MALLY LARGER THAN THE OTHER   Is it because
one of my balls is abnormally larger than the other?

A WHOLE-ASS ADULT   No, it's not that. I really just
came to shower.

A COCK GOBLIN, ONE OF HIS BALLS IS ABNOR-
MALLY LARGER THAN THE OTHER   Liar!
You came here to do what we all come here to do, but
you don't like me.
I bet anything I'm gonna see you later out here with
another guy.
Someone with a more modest testicle, a more reasonable
nut,
And I'm going to be so mad.

A WHOLE-ASS ADULT   I promise this has nothing to
do with your one giant ball.
I just feel filthy right now and nobody in my city has fixed
our water yet.

THE PRESENTER   "Room 56, your time is up. Room 56, please come upstairs to return your key."

A COCK GOBLIN, ONE OF HIS BALLS IS ABNOR- MALLY LARGER THAN THE OTHER   That's me. I gotta go, but if I ever see you again and you don't suck my dick, I'll know you lied today. That'll make you liar. And you're going to have to live with yourself.

A COCK GOBLIN, ONE OF HIS BALLS IS ABNORMALLY LARGER THAN THE OTHER *exits.*

A WHOLE-ASS ADULT   . . . Okay.

THE PRESENTER   And a Whole-Ass Adult enters the shower.
The water goes from cool to warm to hot and reminds him of his mother's baths.
She was the first naked person he ever saw.
Now, there are other people here, naked.
Who came to get clean, to do things others think are dirty.
In the shower next to him, a man is scrubbing off lube from his hand, wrist, and forearm.
Imagine putting that much appendage in someone?
No, really. Do it right now.
While this guy showers.
Imagine being so inside someone you can feel their pulse from inside their rectum.
Imagine trusting someone so much you risk the potential of being emptied by the fistful, you risk them punching straight through your tissue.
Imagine that much trust.
Imagine trusting anyone so much you empty your guts.
You flush all your guts with water, so someone can fill them up with themselves.

Imagine spilling your guts so someone can rearrange your
guts.
Spilling your guts is just an expression,
But I think someone can rearrange your guts. I'll have to
look that up.
According to Tim Dean, / the d—

IT HAS BEEN A VERY HARD WEEK *enters the shower area
with his little fuck-'n'-go bag. He takes out a Fleet and some
Gun Oil. The club music insists on itself.*

THE PRESENTER   (*Surprised.*) Oh. Oh no. No no no.
I was telling because I don't think we should show in this
part!
We shouldn't show this—

IT HAS BEEN A VERY HARD WEEK   Oh, please,
then, tell some more.

THE PRESENTER   (*New possibility.*) Oh. Uh. (*And
what he tells, happens.*) And a Whole-Ass Adult ends his
shower. Clean. He sees this handsome man, an enema
bottle in his hand. This handsome man, he's had a
very hard week, so he fills himself with Fleet. Here, beauty,
risk, a chance.

IT HAS BEEN A VERY HARD WEEK   (*To* A WHOLE-
ASS ADULT.) You come here often?

A WHOLE-ASS ADULT   No, I've never cum here.

IT HAS BEEN A VERY HARD WEEK   So, it's your first
time coming?

A WHOLE-ASS ADULT   No, I've cum before. Just not
here.

IT HAS BEEN A VERY HARD WEEK   Oh. What
brought you here?

A WHOLE-ASS ADULT   I just came out here to get
clean. Why do you come here?

IT HAS BEEN A VERY HARD WEEK   I wanted to
remember my friends.

A WHOLE-ASS ADULT   And did you?

IT HAS BEEN A VERY HARD WEEK   I did.

A WHOLE-ASS ADULT   And now?

IT HAS BEEN A VERY HARD WEEK   And now I want
more than the past. I want a whole load of futures in me.
So I'm cleaning my hole out.

A WHOLE-ASS ADULT   I hope for future loads in me,
too.

THE PRESENTER   (*Hesitant.*) No.

IT HAS BEEN A VERY HARD WEEK   Here, then. (IT
HAS BEEN A VERY HARD WEEK *takes an extra Fleet from his
bag.*) You're welcome to join me.

A WHOLE-ASS ADULT   Thank you.

THE PRESENTER   (*Entranced. He's no longer control-
ling. He's describing.*) A Whole-Ass Adult and It Has
Been a Very Hard Week lube themselves up. They lie
down and insert their Fleets. In Fleet pose, with one
another.

IT HAS BEEN A VERY HARD WEEK   You'll want the
water to run as far into you as it can.
You'll repeat this again two or three more times, depending on how much you'd like inside you. Depending on
how much fiber you take.

A WHOLE-ASS ADULT   Oh, thanks for the tip. I
usually just do one.

IT HAS BEEN A VERY HARD WEEK   Sure thing. I
work at a hospice. Sometimes we do this for our patients.
To help them with blockage. Sometimes we do this to
make the dying a cleaner thing. Less to pick up after.

A WHOLE-ASS ADULT   Doesn't that make this feel
weird for you?

IT HAS BEEN A VERY HARD WEEK   Not really. I'm
always practicing to die.

A WHOLE-ASS ADULT   Is that what it will feel like in
here?

IT HAS BEEN A VERY HARD WEEK   Like you're
dying? When it's really good, on your worst day, yes.
Mostly it just feels like cleaning your hole and waiting
for someone to appreciate it.

A WHOLE-ASS ADULT   Like cleaning tripitas or panza
before you cook it.

IT HAS BEEN A VERY HARD WEEK   Yes, something
like that. Something like getting clean to be eaten. I like to
think it's getting cleaned to take. Even when I bottom, I
tell people my hole fucks them. I grip tight around them
and I say that I am the one doing.

And eventually if you say it long enough, only the really good ones stick around.

A WHOLE-ASS ADULT   I like that. Thank you.
How long should I hold the water until I'm clean clean?

IT HAS BEEN A VERY HARD WEEK   Until you need to go. There's toilets right there.

A WHOLE-ASS ADULT   Thank you. I appreciate the conversation.

IT HAS BEEN A VERY HARD WEEK   Sure thing. My pleasure.

A WHOLE-ASS ADULT   Oh—I think, I think I gotta go.

IT HAS BEEN A VERY HARD WEEK   You go ahead. Gonna hold my water for a bit longer.

A WHOLE-ASS ADULT   Okay. This was nice. I'm Daniel.

IT HAS BEEN A VERY HARD WEEK   It has been, Daniel. I'm Shaun.

IT HAS BEEN A VERY HARD WEEK *is now* SHAUN *and* A WHOLE-ASS ADULT *is now* DANIEL. DANIEL *exits.* SHAUN *remains.*

THE PRESENTER   Oh. Oh no, you
You guys shouldn't have names here. This is just hypo-thetical, so—(*Crisis management.*)
And they both leave!

SHAUN   Oh. It's time.

SHAUN *leaves.*

THE PRESENTER   Thank you guys for that um—(*His notes. Oh god. What's in here?*) Um . . .

LONGTIME PUBLIC-SPEAKING TEACHER MX. VASQUEZ   The subject seems to be getting away from you. Do you need some time to /perhaps collect your thoughts—

THE PRESENTER   No! No no—I got this! Control!
Certainty! Authority!
I'm Laura Linney.
I'm Laura Linney.
I am Laura Linney! I've got this—
As I was saying, the / bathhouse represents for many a bygone marker of community, of connection—

CARLOS *enters.*

CARLOS   Hey.
Hey.
Hello. Hey, dude.
Are you okay? You good?
Um. Were you parTying, too?
Hello?

THE PRESENTER   Me?

CARLOS   Yeah . . . Sorry. I don't mean to be weird.

THE PRESENTER   Oh, no, no, no—I'm not here. I'm not partying. I'm telling, so I'm not here. I've got a time limit / and I think

CARLOS   You're really sexy.

THE PRESENTER   No.

. . .

I mean, that's really kind of you. But no. Thank you.

CARLOS   Sure thing. Oh, I don't work here, by the
way.

THE PRESENTER   Okay. (*Pivot. Impossibly now trying
to do a public-speaking presentation in a bathhouse.*) What
I have found in doing this thesis presentation is / that
nostalgia—

CARLOS   I know the uniform is throwing you off, but I
don't work here. Just tonight. But I don't.

THE PRESENTER   (*Nervous. Danger, and the promise of
delight.*) So you're technically on the clock tonight, then!
So you should go! In My Research, I have found—

From off, somewhere else in the bathhouse, we hear CHELA.

CHELA   CARLOS! ARE YOU TRYING TO FUCK
THAT MAN?!

CARLOS   No, ma'am!

CHELA *enters, looking increasingly snatched.*

CHELA   I told you not to fuck anybody! I'm gonna beat
the shit out of you! I swear to god!

THE PRESENTER   Yes, please beat him. This fuckin'
presentation—is not going great. Goddamn it.

CHELA   I want to sit. I just want to sit down.
I want to sit my ass down right here,

I want a forty. Maybe a Micky's or a King Cobra and no cellulite.
One of these days I wanna have so much fuckin' money and good nylon stockings.
The ones with that line running down the leg. And a good heel.
And I would come here, to a place like this, but for ladies, cuz they don't let us in here except on Tuesdays and even then, / muy apenas

THE PRESENTER   No, we already covered your interiority. This is a presentation about a landscape and it's a very relaxing landscape, so Chela leaves!

CHELA   And I would spread my legs
Spread myself, this ass, right on top of the tile in the sauna
I'd spread my legs—

THE PRESENTER   (*His* ATTENDANT *voice emerges.*)
"Chela, we need you to do another pass of the hot tub area, please! The bears are eating ass in there again and we don't want any more cases of giardia or shigellosis. Now. Please. Let's go. Thank YOU!"

CHELA   Asshole.

CHELA *leaves.* CARLOS *and* THE PRESENTER *remain.*

THE PRESENTER   "Again, we need all custodial to the hot tub area for scat / management."

CARLOS   I told you. I don't work here. And I don't think you really want me to go. Otherwise, I'd be gone, right? That's how / this works?

THE PRESENTER   I hate this so much. Anyway, there is no sex slide here, okay. So, you can just go!

CARLOS   Relax, dude.

THE BATHHOUSE SAYS *speaks.*

THE BATHOUSE SAYS   Relax. It's okay. Relax.

THE PRESENTER   I am! I wanted to, I just wanted to
explain here that—
Can
Can you / go?!

CARLOS   You really are very cute.
When you're nervous. / So cute.

THE PRESENTER   What? No—
Slide / please

CARLOS   Wait.

The slide does not go.

THE PRESENTER   Um . . . / Sli—

CARLOS   Do you want to come—

THE PRESENTER   No. No, I don't. What I want is for
you to let me finish—

THE BATHOUSE SAYS   You don't. Relax. Just relax.

CARLOS   Oh, it's okay, if you don't want to. Do anything. All good. You're cute, though. I hope you actually
know that.

THE PRESENTER   Thank you. So
So are . . . y—eah. Yeah. Thanks.

CARLOS   Why are you here?

THE PRESENTER   Because I go to this school and this is a presentation / and—

CARLOS   This is ideation; a fantasy, at best, but go off. I think imagination is sexy.

THE PRESENTER   Why are you still here?!

CARLOS   Just to fuck. To feel, more or less, y'know?

THE PRESENTER   I don't.

CARLOS   Clearly. You could / if—

THE PRESENTER   It seems like you got what you wanted already, so you should go home! (*A flimsy pivot.*) Okay, / sli—

CARLOS   I can't. Too far. I just flew in tonight, years ago, from Boston.
I'm not from there. I'm from Texas, but I flew to Los Angeles years ago, and I needed somewhere to feel safe. Alive.

THE PRESENTER   So, you came here?

CARLOS   Yes.
On the way here, at the Logan airport, I was waiting for my flight at the bar, bored,
And then there was my hometown, on the news, on all these screens.
I watched this man, on television, enter a Wal-Mart with an assault rifle.
He drove almost twelve hours to my hometown in Texas,

to this Wal-Mart my mom loves, to shoot the Mexican
clean off it.
He killed twenty-three people in my hometown, at a
Wal-Mart there, years ago, to help clean his country.
I watched it happen at the airport in Boston, and people
just rolled their bags through, like the world wasn't
ending.
And when I got here, when I landed here in LA, years
ago, being alive didn't make sense.
So, I came here, to the North Hollywood Spa, because
it's the closest thing I have to a home in any city I visit.
Always almost the same in every city. The mirrors, this
maze. And no history of bullets. Not like a school, or a
gay bar, or a Wal-Mart.
I came here to be almost home because my home was just
bodies and bullets and television screens.

THE PRESENTER   You felt safe here?

CARLOS   Enough, I think?
I think I wanted to die here? I can't remember.
I think I'm crashing. The comedown is always weird.
It was hours ago, in these hallways, years ago, this short,
stout Filipino daddy, so sweet, he calls me in, and I'm not
ready to bottom, but who ever is after a national tragedy?
He fills me in this room, with himself, he feeds me little
clouds from his little glass pipe, blows clouds on my skin,
kisses them into me, and there I am, in that room, full of
clouds in my lungs and this beautiful man inside me, like
his dick was the only thing binding my bones together.
I am here, years ago, full of all the things that I've been
told will kill me, and tonight, they are the only things to
possibly keep me alive tomorrow, years ago, in this place.
Is that why you like it here?

THE PRESENTER   . . . At . . . At school?

CARLOS   In the past. In this place you've never been.

THE PRESENTER   You should probably go. You have
rooms to finish, right?

CARLOS   And myself. Are you sure you don't want to
come?

THE PRESENTER   Where?

CARLOS   Wherever you want.

THE PRESENTER   I—

CARLOS   No pressure. I'll be around.
Should I go now? Do you need me / to go?

THE PRESENTER   (*No.*) Yes. Um . . . "Uh, we need
custodial in / the hot tub—"

CARLOS   (*Yes, Daddy.*)   Yessir.
See ya around.

CARLOS *exits.* THE PRESENTER *gets hard and covers himself
in the most mortifying way possible.*

THE PRESENTER   Oh god. Actually, can we just pause
for a little bit? I really need to
I've had to
use the bathroom so bad this whole presentation.
Can someone just take over for a little bit? SLIDE!

THE PRESENTER *rushes out to the bathroom with the sad-
dest boner. From elsewhere enters* THE BATH BEAUTY,
dazzling!

THE BATH BEAUTY
Here she is, world!
Here she is, boys!

Slide

Slide 13

From darkness, unintelligible bottom noises, horrifying and hungry. The sound of furious bottoms turns into cheers and applause. The doll, the diva, THE BATH BEAUTY *emerges with a microphone and a gorgeous cocktail!*

THE BATH BEAUTY   Here's Googie Gomez! Oh, wrong bathhouse! I'm joshin' ya! That's an old, gay joke! Ya love me for it! Oh, boys! It feels so special to be here again and always with you, on these floors, in the walls! God, you boys are so beautiful.
Now, just last week I asked Joe, I said, "Joe, baby, and what about that sweet man that you used to bring around here?" And Joe says, he says, "Oh, you know how men are. One day they're here and the next." And that's all he said. So, I'm gonna sing for you. This is the song where people get up and leave to do what you do! The attention span is so short here. What's a dick anyway? It only takes a song, right?

She sings "My Man." SHAUN *enters, and with him, his private room.* THE PRESENTER *hurries in with a sad little stain on his pants.*

THE PRESENTER   Oh, no, no, fuck no! WE ARE IN THE MILIEU OF—/ Slide, please!

SHAUN   Hey, guy, look, I'm gonna ask you, and I mean this kindly. I come here because it's quieter than the bars. Could you keep it down, for just a bit—

THE PRESENTER   No! This is my presentation and I / want to finish—

SHAUN   You can watch if you'd like, though. You can watch what happens next. Would you like to?

THE PRESENTER   . . . No / I—

SHAUN   Do you want to?

THE PRESENTER   Yes.

SHAUN   Quiet, then. Just watch. We are in room 15, in the hallways downstairs. This is my private room. Where I come to fuck, and where I come to sleep when I don't fuck and there are no ghosts in this room. They're always cruising. Ghosts hate closed doors—

DANIEL *enters.*

DANIEL   Hey, sorry to interrupt you—

SHAUN   Oh, don't sweat it.

DANIEL   So . . . did, did you—

SHAUN   Not yet, no. Did you—

DANIEL   No, not yet.

SHAUN   That's how it goes here, some Thursday nights into Friday mornings into Sunday evenings.

DANIEL   It feels that way. Late and early. It feels like a long time ago right now.
It feels like we happened a long time ago.

SHAUN   We did. We're going to happen again. We just have to wait. That's the best part of coming, is waiting.

DANIEL   It's fun. All these hallways.

SHAUN   It's a funhouse.

DANIEL   It's a silly name. Bathhouse. It's silly. Things live in houses. Nothing lives here.

SHAUN   Some people do. Cheaper than a hotel. Better than a sidewalk. Shit, I've been coming here long enough to feel like I live here.

DANIEL   You seem like it.

SHAUN   Old?

DANIEL   No, like you live here.

SHAUN   Sad?

DANIEL   Comfortable.

SHAUN   I am.

DANIEL   I like it here.

SHAUN   I do too.

DANIEL   Can I join you?

SHAUN   Here, in the room?

DANIEL   Yes.

SHAUN   Sure.

DANIEL   Thanks. (DANIEL *sits next to* SHAUN. *He lifts his hand to place it on* SHAUN*'s thigh. Before he does:*) May I?

SHAUN   Sure. That feels nice. You have nice hands.

DANIEL   I think they feel rough.

SHAUN   They do. I like that. You work?

DANIEL   At Wal-Mart, yeah. I unload trucks.

SHAUN   They feel good. The work on your hands. It's nice.

DANIEL   . . . I like . . .
Your thighs

SHAUN   Okay. (DANIEL *grabs* SHAUN*'s dick.* SHAUN *melts into it.* SHAUN *lifts his hand to touch* DANIEL*'s thigh.*) May— (DANIEL *grabs* SHAUN*'s hand and pulls it toward his balls.*) Oh.

DANIEL   Sorry.

SHAUN   No, this feels—You feel great.

DANIEL   So do you.

SHAUN   Do you like verbal?

DANIEL   What?

SHAUN   Dirty talk.

DANIEL   Sure.

SHAUN   Wanna tell me something sexy?

DANIEL   Uh—
Yeah. Um—

SHAUN   You get nervous?

DANIEL   Talking, yeah. I don't wanna sound silly . . .
. . . I like your . . . dick. It feels nice.
It's a big dick.
You like when I touch your fat—

SHAUN   (*Stifling laughter.*) Not quite, man. Here. Close
your eyes. I'll close mine.
Tell me a story. I'll tell you one, too.

With eyes closed, SHAUN *and* DANIEL *stroke each other
through this scene.*

DANIEL   I had this co-worker, he was older.
We were unloading a truck once.

SHAUN   I had a lover once, he was older.
We fucked wild here once.

DANIEL   My co-worker. He was married and mean,
And he smelled like my dad's compadres.
I wanted to bury myself between his legs.

SHAUN   I was mean and we weren't married,
But he smelled like Aspen and cigar
I wanted to bury myself between his legs too.

DANIEL   He'd piss out back sometimes, outside,

when we were unloading, and my neck would get hot.
I wanted to see him piss.

SHAUN   He'd piss on my back sometimes, inside
sometimes
before he'd leave his loads in me. God, I wanted anything I
could get from him.

DANIEL   And one time, I got curious, so
So I went to piss next to him, but he was just standing
there.
Hard in his own hand. Waiting.

SHAUN   Hard. I'd wait for him here.
At the end of the night, when he'd had enough of everyone else here.
He was so tired some nights. So I'd just lie here, sleeping
next to him.

DANIEL   I touched him.
Just like this. Just like this.

SHAUN   Just like that. Oh, fuck yeah.
God. I'd touch him just like this.

DANIEL   Fuck. Oh, god.

SHAUN   Yeah? Keep going.

DANIEL   And I kept touching him, and I bent over
quickly
I put him in my mouth

SHAUN   I miss him in my mouth.
I miss touching him, being bent over.
Keep going.

DANIEL   It was quick. It was really quick.
But he tasted like I made sense.
And just as quick he pulled away.

SHAUN   It was quick. It was really quick.
It didn't make sense. He was here once.
And it seemed so quick when he went away.

DANIEL   And he got meaner and wouldn't speak to me
after that
And that night, I just smelled him on my mouth, and I
swear
I've never wanted anything more than to drink him whole
on my four legs.
Animal. I've never wanted so bad to knock someone to the
ground and lap them up.

SHAUN   And he never came back, and I got meaner,
And at night I would miss him, and I never wished I'd
kept someone so bad.
He went so fast, his body, all of it went. I was furious and
I wanted him.
I wished I'd kept him clamped shut in me and saved him,
kept him inside me.

DANIEL   Fuck. (DANIEL *growls, hungry; he cums.*)

SHAUN   Fuck. (SHAUN *growls, hungry; he cums.*)

DANIEL   And now.

SHAUN   Waiting. Until we can go again. But you're
welcome to stay here. While everything ends. I'd like
you to.

DANIEL   I'd like to. I'd like to stay here.

SHAUN   When you are older, I'd like you to remember me here, yeah?

DANIEL   So long as the place stands, yes.

SHAUN   And if it doesn't, so long, then.
But not for now. For now, us. This.

They wait with each other. THE BATH BEAUTY *finishes the remainder of "My Man."*

THE BATH BEAUTY   Thank you! Thank you all so much! Such sweet, sweet hearts. Now, I know a lot of you boys don't know me, but I just want to thank you for giving me an audience!

THE PRESENTER   (*Full of what he's seen. Terrified of being in love with it.*) Oh god.

THE BATH BEAUTY   (*To* THE PRESENTER.) I've never met god, but I think I got close in here once. That's what I would feel like. Like Venus right here.
Propped up on that little stoop over the hot tub.
Champagne and gin and whiskey flowing,
And all these little cherubs in towels ushering me in.
It would smell like mint and eucalyptus.
It wasn't here. Not in this place, exactly.
But this place is everywhere. Was.
I'm telling you because we thought the world was just starting back then, too.
It felt like we were on the verge of something big! It felt like we were about to happen!
And then the boys started going, and coming less, and city government thought this little heaven wasn't heavenly.

THE PRESENTER   Why—
Why are you telling me this?

THE BATH BEAUTY   I'm telling you because we
thought the world was ending back then, too. Just like
it feels right now. Doesn't it always? Can't you feel it?

THE PRESENTER   (*The weight of how true it feels. The
terror of that end, of that beginning. That possibility.*) No
more. No more of this. No!
We're done. No more showing! No More!
Slide! (*The slide doesn't go. He commands.*)
No! We are today! We are today, in linoleum and bells
that are too loud and cafeteria trays and scoreboards and
lockers and alone and alone and and and—
(*He begs.*) SLIDE!
PLEASE!
(*Desperate. Heartbroken. Monstrous!*)
SLIDE!!!!!!!

And SHAUN *and* DANIEL *go away. And* THE BATH BEAUTY
*vanishes. The bathhouse retreats. The ugly cafetorium
returns.*

Slide

Slide 14

Anxiety, shame, and hydrotherapy.

THE PRESENTER   (*Mechanical and desperate to end.*)
As I was saying, from the murders of three women by
George Joseph Smith in their bathtubs to the infamous
shower scene in *Psycho,* baths invoke a landscape that
screams, "You can die here at any moment!" just as swiftly
as "Oh, a lavender bath bomb! Now I won't drown my
kids!"

Similarly, bathhouses promise guests will be DP'ed by
relaxation and terror, anxiety attached to pleasure at the
frenulum. From the Continental Baths to Steamworks,
these defunct places were funhouses of fuckery. In my
extensive research for this PowerPoint—

STRONG PICK-ME ENERGY *enters.*

STRONG PICK-ME ENERGY   Um, actually, sorry, I
don't want to call you out or anything, but I would like to
call you in by calling attention to some of the holes in this.
This all seems poorly put together.

THE PRESENTER   Do you want to do this?

STRONG PICK-ME ENERGY   Oh, no. Absolutely not.
I just want to uplift that you're kind of shitting the bed.
Thematically. Mx. Vasquez, I'm still really curious about

the specifics of the assignment here. This is supposed to be
An Informative Presentation, correct?

LONGTIME PUBLIC-SPEAKING TEACHER MX. VASQUEZ
descends! Hallelujah! A body!

LONGTIME PUBLIC-SPEAKING TEACHER MX.
VASQUEZ   Oh, shit. I'm still here? Yes, an informative
presentation, which means it cannot be persuasive, so we
can't give our opinions to the audience.

STRONG PICK-ME ENERGY   This doesn't feel very
informative.

LONGTIME PUBLIC-SPEAKING TEACHER MX.
VASQUEZ   That's your opinion. So, that's persuasive.
I'm persuaded by that statement. Good work.

STRONG PICK-ME ENERGY   Thank you. I really
appreciate you. And all the work you've done this semester. During these unprecedented times. I'm just curious if
the speaker could tell us why they chose this topic. It just
seems like a really odd topic to choose for a tenth-grade
honors presentation.

LONGTIME PUBLIC-SPEAKING TEACHER MX.
VASQUEZ   Yeah, what is up with that?
What's up WITH that?
What the fuck, gurl?
It's really not giving, mawmaw.
What's tea, flop?
Okay, I'm done being relatable.
(*To* THE PRESENTER.) What's up with this thing? Do you
care to explain?

THE PRESENTER   You said we should speak about a
subject we care about.

LONGTIME PUBLIC-SPEAKING TEACHER MX.
VASQUEZ   So you chose . . . bathhouses?

THE PRESENTER   . . . Why do you care so much?

LONGTIME PUBLIC-SPEAKING TEACHER MX.
VASQUEZ   Excuse me?

THE PRESENTER   Why does it matter why I chose this
topic?

LONGTIME PUBLIC-SPEAKING TEACHER MX.
VASQUEZ   Because you're a tenth grader!

THE PRESENTER   Who is being played by an adult!
(THE PRESENTER *is in fact an adult. This is a play, after
all, and the only fiction I can muster is flimsy.*)
An adult who is a pervert!
A pervert fascinated by extinction!
By Armageddons!
One day these things were and then they were gone and
nobody seems to miss them!
Isn't that important?

STRONG PICK-ME ENERGY   I did my presentation
on Bolivia. If you need a break maybe I can present. Mx.
Vasquez, I'll just do my presentation now.
Ahem "Nestled in the enchanted mountains of a land long
forgotten by man, Bolivia represents the magic of—"

THE PRESENTER   God, will you shut up, you fucking
try-hard! Nobody cares about your goddamn presentation
on Bolivia! It doesn't matter! You're going to be very
successful and get an A in speech and work for Monsanto
Homeland Security Hulu someday and either way you'll
still end up sucking dick behind a Panda Express like the
rest of us because there's nowhere else to go if you can't

host, (*His* ATTENDANT *voice breaks through.*) "so just sit
down and shut the fuck up, or we'll have you escorted
out!"

STRONG PICK-ME ENERGY *immediately cums.*

STRONG PICK-ME ENERGY   You . . . you can't talk
to me that way.
My father runs a very powerful tear-gas-canister start-up
and my mom works for Free-Form.
We have lawyers!

STRONG PICK-ME ENERGY *exits.*

LONGTIME PUBLIC-SPEAKING TEACHER MX.
VASQUEZ   Wow. Okay, there we go! That's it. That's
a voice!

THE PRESENTER   I'm sorry—

LONGTIME PUBLIC-SPEAKING TEACHER MX.
VASQUEZ   No apologizing. That's the thing with public
speaking, is mistakes are going to happen and you can't let
the audience know. Audiences don't know any better. And
that's the thing with better, is we never get to it in history.
History is full of mistakes and claims poorly researched and
anxiety. And that's the thing classrooms and bathhouses
are full of. People being horny about their own anxieties
in concert with those of others. And THAT is what public
speaking is all about, what being public is all about.
You remind me so much of myself, years ago. This place.

THE PRESENTER   This school?

LONGTIME PUBLIC-SPEAKING TEACHER MX.
VASQUEZ   Oh, hun, it's not a school anymore. Got shut

down by the state years ago, after they fired all the homos.
Look around.

*And it is no longer a cafetorium/classroom, but the bones of
one. It is abandoned too. It is a foreclosed building.*

THE PRESENTER   Oh. / Yes.

LONGTIME PUBLIC-SPEAKING TEACHER MX.
VASQUEZ   Yes. This shithole. It's scheduled for demolition next week, and tomorrow, and tomorrow, and you
keep trespassing here to obsess about what it was once.
Before this. And thank god, because I can remember, now,
what I was here.

THE PRESENTER   My teacher?

LONGTIME PUBLIC-SPEAKING TEACHER MX.
VASQUEZ   Before that, sweetie. "Locker or room?"

THE PRESENTER   You worked here? When / it was . . .

LONGTIME PUBLIC-SPEAKING TEACHER MX.
VASQUEZ   A bathhouse. Yes. And I didn't work here,
kid. I ran this place. My voice ran these halls. Sounded like
yours did just now.

LONGTIME PUBLIC-SPEAKING TEACHER MX. VASQUEZ
compels the voice from the ATTENDANT. *Witchcraft.*

THE PRESENTER   "Lockers are $35 if you're not a
member." (*The clarity is surprising, the power in it.*) Whoa.

LONGTIME PUBLIC-SPEAKING TEACHER MX.
VASQUEZ   Just like that. This place, it'll do that you.
It'll make you want control. Certainty.

THE PRESENTER   Authority. "Okay, I'm gonna buzz you in, and we'll keep your ID till you bring your key back."

LONGTIME PUBLIC-SPEAKING TEACHER MX. VASQUEZ   It feels good to begin the world for someone, doesn't it?

THE PRESENTER   . . . Yes.

LONGTIME PUBLIC-SPEAKING TEACHER MX. VASQUEZ   It feels good to end the world for someone too.

THE PRESENTER   "Locker 90, your time is up! Locker 90, please turn in your key."

LONGTIME PUBLIC-SPEAKING TEACHER MX. VASQUEZ   It is the wildest thing inside you. That feeling.

THE PRESENTER   It's lonely.

LONGTIME PUBLIC-SPEAKING TEACHER MX. VASQUEZ   It's power. Over pleasure.
It's why they came here, hungry for pilgrimage. Begging for permission to be.

THE PRESENTER   To be what?

LONGTIME PUBLIC-SPEAKING TEACHER MX. VASQUEZ   Anything. Lovers. Strangers. Nameless mounds of flesh clumped together on a couch. Heads leaning into shoulders, on chests. Sweet swans and goblins blurring into one another. They came here to be anything they couldn't say they were out there, to live everything they couldn't live out there. And I rang them up. Watched them come in and become nothing together.

Then I watched them leave. Watched the sunlight turn
them back into themselves.
It's a dangerous thing. Too much possibility. And they did
nothing with it out there. All of it squandered on what?
Selfish faggots who hoarded their pleasure.
It's why these things needed to end.

THE PRESENTER   But these places could have been so
much more!

LONGTIME PUBLIC-SPEAKING TEACHER MX.
VASQUEZ   But they weren't! I can't tell you how many
times I turned away trans women right at the door. We
had posters that said "No Girls Allowed!" like it was cute!
Turned away men we said couldn't pass for themselves too.
Turned away people we called family.
Some house, right?
And it feels like nobody learned anything some days. How
cruel we were to each other here sometimes too. This
wasn't paradise either, kid.
What place could be?
And still, I miss it. It misses itself. / My god, I miss myself.

THE BATHHOUSE SAYS   My god, I miss myself,
My god, my mirrors,
Every door, my mouth,
Every hall, my hole,
Every way to let up,
Every way to cum in /
My god, I miss me.

THE PRESENTER   (*In séance, with* THE BATHHOUSE
SAYS) My god, I miss me.
(*And now himself, and the pleasure of having not been.*)
Oh, shit. I remember / it—

LONGTIME PUBLIC-SPEAKING TEACHER MX.
VASQUEZ *is now* JUST VASQUEZ.

JUST VASQUEZ   You don't. It's not memory.

THE PRESENTER   Oh. Oh, I feel / it—

JUST VASQUEZ   YES! That's it! This place, just like any
of us, it longs to be longed for! Yes!

DANIEL *enters. The showers return.*

DANIEL   Hey, do you know, if—
If we wanted to stay longer, could we?

THE PRESENTER   (THE ATTENDANT *voice breaks
through, flirting, laying it on.*) "We can extend your locker
four more hours for $15. I can make it 10 for you, chulo."
Oh god! No, sorry!

*The walls vibrate; the ghost of Bette Midler's "Friends" slowed
and reverbed comes through. The lights flicker.*

THE PRESENTER   That music?

SHAUN *enters; his private room enters with him.*

SHAUN   That's the old bones of this place. That's what
they sound like when they're rattled. Like music, while
waiting. "Cuz you gotta have friends." God, I miss them.
God, I miss me.

DANIEL   I'll remember you. (*To* THE PRESENTER.) Can
I please get more time?

THE PRESENTER   No, let / me—

CARLOS *enters, still uniformed, backed by mirrors.*

CARLOS   Hey, boss daddy, one of the glory holes has
a bunch of Crisco on it. Do we have any cleaner that's
special for Crisco? / How do I get it off?

CHELA *enters, trailed by a St. Andrew's cross; another wall of mirrors too.*

CHELA   Are you fucking kidding me? ¡¿Otra vez!? Ay, no, como me chingan el alma, pinches jotos! Ya tengan piedad, por / el favor de dios!

CARLOS   I know! J-Lube is so much better! I guess Crisco is kinda retro, / so it makes sense.

DANIEL   (*To* THE PRESENTER.) You think I could take you up on the discount, then, papi? I'd really / like to—

SHAUN   (*To* DANIEL.*)* We used to sit right on that couch, in our towels, sometimes, just watching the news, holding each other / until—

THE PRESENTER   CAN YOU ALL PLEASE JUST LET ME FINISH! Please!
Sorry—

JUST VASQUEZ   Stop apologizing.

CHELA   And get to the pinche point! I need this shift to end! It's time!

CARLOS   The pinche point so we can finally get to the fucking!

THE PRESENTER   What's the point, since you all know every fucking thing!?

A shower emerges.

SHAUN   (*And now, a timeless daddy. A tender daddy-ing. The thesis.*) To question nostalgia, and think of mourning as a joyful thing. To consecrate all the places and people nobody took the time to remember. To remember all the best times we made here, the possibilities, fleeting and tender. So, to imagine, and then move on. That's the thing we did best here, was remember. And then let go.

JUST VASQUEZ   And the best way to let go is just let the audience picture you naked. So, you can just let go now. Tell us. How did we all get here?

THE PRESENTER *undresses, gets in the shower. Naked, he begins.*

THE PRESENTER   Debris. Rubble. Longing. Envy. (*Slowly, slowly, from the shower, time travel. Morphing. All his times collapsing, shimmering through his throat, in his bones.*) We are in the milieu of last
Last
Last
Last last last week.
Years ago,
I am assigned a presentation.
Really, this is what I want to do though.
I want to hurl myself through a mirror and hope time can be cut across that way.
I am in tenth grade. Not now, of course. Then. I don't want to be.
I want to be 1970s and 1980s, but I've never been any of those things.
I was an eighth grader when I first read about bathhouses; they were all gone by then.
By the time I am a ninth grader I have a man I call my lover and sometimes he tells me stories about places that happened when I was his age.
By the time I am a tenth grader, I don't have time to answer complicated questions about my former lover because I am ugly, so all I've got is young, so I don't have much time.

Butterflies don't live very long. I wonder if they ever think about dinosaurs.

By the time I am an eleventh grader I will have primed myself to long for lovers who will pass, who will pass me around, who will pass me by, and that is the closest I'll have to lineage, is I'll know loss is a kind of love.

So by the time I am the age I am now, by the time I am thirty-something, by the time it is 2052, by this impossible time, I will become a very young ghost haunting the hallways of my adult self, I'll be here and loving a back-then always,

a stain of myself on myself.

And somedays I'll wish I wasn't a body. I'll wish I was a search result, a webpage, a PowerPoint slide. I'll wish myself a Google image, but nerve endings will insist on themselves.

Anyway, by the time I am a tenth grader I am a pervert fascinated with things that end.

So, we are in the milieu of the end of things.

We are wrapping things up. We're almost at the end.

The walls vibrate, rumble, the music, the bones, the ghosts, the lights, all of it pulsing. Yes, not a nostalgia, but a joyous mourning for all the gorgeous darkness that once was. The world returns, just well-lit enough to almost see everyone in this dark room, a summoning.

Into the bathhouse, at the end of the world.

THE PRESENTER   And the beginning.
Slide.

Slide.

Slide 15

CARLOS   And here I'd like you to imagine you are a door. Here, we'd like you to imagine that every opening is a new way in. And to make this right, we have to imagine that our dissonant pleasures can move in concert. Imagine you are a way in. Imagine that on a pitch-black night you possibly saved someone. Imagine the difference between a door and a hallway is reprieve, respite, repose, respair, resurrection.

SHAUN   Imagine through the door all your dead returned. Imagine every pleasure you've taken with the dead and not with their dying. Imagine the last tea dance. Imagine whatever last dance, last chance for love. Imagine yourself young enough to long for what compelled Donna to sing like that. Imagine then, the time you wanted most, the hungriest you ever were.

DANIEL   Imagine that smallest version of yourself, that teenage fury, terrified and terrifying. Imagine all that longing that small person held in their desk, in their body rebelling with and against them, imagine the moment that young person knew touch could feel good. Perhaps it is too much to imagine this. Perhaps it is too much to imagine touch as something that can feel good. I didn't think it possible until just a few moments ago, just a few years from now, just now, when I forgot all over again. Imagine that young person you were once, are. Imagine you are always moments away from the first time your heart broke.

CHELA   Imagine ecstasy was a precipice and you couldn't wait to keep falling. Imagine that fall down below and up into all the things that most beg your lips to part and ah, ooh, unf. Imagine the thing your skin wants most, imagine the want that most makes you weep. Imagine the risk. So, imagine the first time you lingered in the doorway, just on the other side of what might be possible, and imagine someone shooed you away, or said no thanks, man, or worse yet, imagine that first time you were wanted, that first thing you wanted. Imagine the thing that makes you cum hardest, imagine it now, next to someone doing the same, perhaps a stranger.

JUST VASQUEZ   Imagine the worst thing you've done for the thing that makes you cum hardest. We have often been told that audiences do not like to be told what to do. Bratty bottoms, who sit to watch as if passive, only to assert the eye's hunger, to want to be fed, to want to want. We have been told by some studies and theories of relation that self-disclosure is the only way to build a relationship with someone, and perhaps this is why audiences sit in silence; they may want each other. We have been told this is why audiences cannot sit with silence for too long; a pause might indicate to the audience that the speaker does not know what they are talking about.
Ethos is very important, and often ill-defined. Eros too well-oiled to grasp firmly.
So, imagine, again, the thing that makes you cum hardest now.
Imagine you might be honest about what makes you cum next to a stranger, a friend.
The heart gapes to think.
Thankfully, we seldom think with our heart.

The brain is much more capacious when it comes to
breaking.
Breathing. Bending. All the things we long to do next to
someone.

CARLOS   Imagine, instead, your last lover.

SHAUN   Imagine, instead, that your lover lasts.

DANIEL   So, imagine the impossible.

CHELA   Your body at its most everlasting and all that
distance since then.

JUST VASQUEZ   Where else to face this but at these
little temples? Where else might we be bored in such a
shattering way?

THE PRESENTER   I was just curious, is all, about these
places. About what it might have been like?

JUST VASQUEZ   About what it was like here?

THE PRESENTER   About what it might be, to feel less
alone. "Would you like a locker or a room today? Rooms
are—"

JUST VASQUEZ   Oh, sweetie. You can't learn that from
a presentation and you'll hardly know that from the front
desk. You won't know unless you go. Even then, nothing
is guaranteed. It could be hours here. But if you want to
know, I can take your shift.
You should go inside, while the world is cracked open like
this.
"It's free for sad bitches today. I'll buzz you in."

Buzz

CHELA   Por fin. Puta madre. SLIDE!

Slide

Slide 16

Checking in.

THE PRESENTER   Am I . . . I am . . . I am in the milieu of last, / last—

CHELA   No, no, no. No mas pinches milieus. ¡YA! Didn't your teacher say less telling, more showing?! Shut the fuck up! Go look around so I can finish here.

THE PRESENTER   Yes, ma'am. (*He starts to go.*) Um . . . where should I start? / What do I—

CHELA   Ay, dios! SHARLIE!! ¡HIJO DE TU CHING-ADA MADRE! CARLOS, I SWEAR IF YOU WENT TO SUCK / A PEEPEE—

CARLOS *enters again.*

CARLOS   Right here, boss. (*To* THE PRESENTER.) Oh, hey, / you stayed

THE PRESENTER   Hey. Yeah, I did. Um. Would you like to . . . Would it be alright / if you—

CHELA   Ey, he's still on the clock!! ¡Aver, reportate cabrón!

CARLOS   Yes, ma'am! I threw the load of towels and sheets in the wash, and I got the upstairs rooms, too!

CHELA   Good job, Sharlie! And you didn't touch no peepees, right?

CARLOS   You wanna smell my hands?

CHELA   No! How do I know you didn't put a pajarito in your mouth?

CARLOS   Do you want to smell my breath?

CHELA   No, cochino! Don't be a nasty. Okay, pos then, that's it. You're done.

CARLOS   Are you proud of me?

CHELA   No.

CARLOS   Oh.

CHELA   I'm not mad either. I'm exhausted. But this is just work. It's hard to be proud of work.

THE PRESENTER   This is a lot of work. I didn't know.

CHELA   Yup. It is.

CARLOS   Did I do good? Can I fuck now?

CHELA   You can do whatever you want. I'm not your fucking mom.

CARLOS   Thank you. (CARLOS *removes his uniform. He grabs a clean towel from the cart. Then, to* THE PRESENTER.) Shift's done. I can show you around.

CHELA   Ey, Sharlie, before you go, you like it here?

CARLOS   It's cleaner than the Slammer. And it's way cleaner than the Zone.

CHELA   I clean this place very good. But do you like how you feel here, Sharlie? You like all the men here running around being crazy boys?

CARLOS   I like when people want me here.

CHELA   People are going to want you for a good while. When you're young, that's how it goes.

CARLOS   Yeah. Can I still get a ride? After?

CHELA   You can get a ride to Chatsworth.

CARLOS   I'll take it.

CHELA   Good. Do you need money?

CARLOS   No. It's okay. I got it.

CHELA   You're a liar. You're a bad liar, too. Why are all of you such bad liars?

CARLOS   Habit. I'm going to go fuck now.

CHELA   I'm going to embarrass you over the loudspeaker when it's time to go. I'm gonna tell everyone you got cuts in your butt. (*To* THE PRESENTER.) You really wanna be in here with a nasty peepee boy with a cut-up butt?

THE PRESENTER   (*Thrilled for what's to come. Smitten.*) It could be worse.

CHELA   Ugh. Oye, Sharlie, the steam room, is it—

CARLOS   Yup. Empty. And clean. I put the wet-floor sign outside. And I taped the little "Out of Order" sign outside the door.

CHELA   Ay, Sharlie. You're really good at this. "You keep this up, you might own this place one day."

CARLOS   "Aww, thanks, boss. That's the dream."

CHELA   Shut up, Sharlie. That's not a good dream. Be safe y mucho cuidado. I'm going to take my break. (*To* THE PRESENTER.) Y tú, pórtate bien, nene. Me lo cuidas, Sharlie.

CARLOS   Yes, ma'am.

THE PRESENTER   (*To* CARLOS.) Come.

THE PRESENTER *enters the bathhouse with* CARLOS. *They exit.*

Steam

Slide Missing

There are no slides here. Just CHELA *relaxing.*
She enters the sauna, carrying a beautiful towel and a cute
bag of toiletries.
She removes her work uniform.
There is steam everywhere.
She rubs oils on her body.
The heat feels good. Her muscles unknot.
She spreads her legs.
She spreads her arms and leans back.
She fills the sauna.
It smells like rose, and mint, and Chanel No. 5.
She breathes in, deep. She exhales.
She leans back and closes her eyes.
A slowed version of Donna Summer's "I Feel Love" plays.
She sings along quietly.
She laughs to herself.
She laughs.
She laughs until she sobs.
My god, she's tired. She sobs until she laughs.
She runs her hands over her body. Every inch of it.
She enjoys herself, this place, the work she's put in.
Then, she speaks.

CHELA   We are in the milieu of last, last, last week.
My god, where does the time go, in a place like this?
In a bathhouse, the time goes in the sauna, by the vending
machine,

on the patio deck, in a little glass pipe, and all that smoke,
my god;
that's where all that time goes,
up your ass with a hose or a bulb.
The time goes on your knees, your worn shoulders,
in the blue-black-purple veins, and your crooked back,
your blistered feet.
And sometimes the time just goes and goes, up in the
clouds,
steams upwards sometimes.
Some times, right?
It takes so very long to do all the things there are to do
here,
so it takes so very long to clean all the things there are to
clean here.
My god.
So much of my life, gone here.
My god.

CHELA *masturbates. A chorus of key rings, and popper
huffing, and breath joins the ghost of Donna Summer's
"I Feel Love." Outside, demolition sounds, crumbling. This
world ends. Outside becomes a parking lot, another Panera,
maybe. But not this room here. Not yet. Just* CHELA *in the
steam. Ecstasy. I feel love.*

END OF PLAY

Acknowledgments

Of course, I owe a tremendous debt of gratitude to Midtowne
Spa in Los Angeles (closed), Midtowne Spa in Austin (closed),
the North Hollywood Spa ("We Never Close"), Steamworks
in Chicago, the Megaplex and the Eagle's Nest in Providence,
and every other place of ill repute I've reached for in this play.

I would not be writing plays without the encouragement,
talents, and mentorship of Victor I. Cazares, Rudy Ramirez,
Rupert Reyes, and Raul Garza, who invited me to theater when
I was primarily a teacher. I write plays thanks to the instruction
and friendship of Nkenna Akunna, Alexa Derman, Julia Jarcho,
and Seayoung Yim. You were the first people to read my baby
pages. You were the first people to let me imagine this play and
then you baptized it (Derman!). This play is yours. Thank you,
too, to Kathy Ng, Dhari Noel, and Ro Reddick, who make me
want to be a better writer. I would not have found my way to
these writers and peers had it not been for the warmth and
friendship of Lucas Baisch and Tatyana-Marie Carlo, who con-
vinced me to say yes to this version of myself. Thanks, y'all!

I owe these pages, too, to the workshop teams that have assembled at Brown and the Flea to give breath and voice to this
play. Their names are listed in the production history of the

play. Find these actors and directors. Hire them. Follow their artistry and work. Thank you all so, so much.

Morgan Jenness, you sorceress, you oracle, you force, you herald, you wonder. Thank you, thank you, thank you. My deepest love to you, for all that you have gifted this play. My deepest gratitude for respair.

This iteration of *Bathhouse.pptx* emerged largely due to the support of the Flea. My deepest gratitude to Martin Meccouri, who has encouraged this play from the beginning, and to Niegel Smith, who has provided unwavering support for this project. Of course, I am thankful, too, for the mentorship, warmth, generosity, and protection of Chay Yew. Thank you all.

My deepest gratitude to Jeremy O. Harris and the readers assembled to adjudicate the Yale Drama Series Prize. What a boon to receive! This is the best graduation present. Thank you. I cannot thank Jessie Kindig, Ash Lago, and Susan Laity at Yale University Press enough for their patience, warmth, and generosity, for modeling the belief that "editing is cultivation and a kind of care work . . . a political craft."

I owe my living to all the people who love me most, in brutal, dazzling, gentle ways. I am thankful for all the ways I have been cared for, protected, and loved by Tala Agunos, Armando Briones, Adrienne Dawes, Johnny Estrella, Eddie Gamboa, Kareem Khubchandani, Ryan Martinez, Michelle Messick, Robert Ramirez, Joshua K. Reason, and Taji Senior. I love you all tremendously. Your friendship, care, and love leave me absolutely undone. Thank you.

Finally, to my parents J Gerardo and Rosa Isela, I love you so much. I owe my world to you both.